CREATIVE IDEAS
FOR
YOUTH EVANGELISM

CREATIVE IDEAS
FOR
YOUTH EVANGELISM

Edited by Nick Aiken

Written by:
Mark Brown, Geoff Read, Patrick Angier,
Mark Melluish, Mike Burns, John Reaney

Marshall Pickering
An Imprint of HarperCollins*Publishers*

Marshall Pickering is an Imprint of
HarperCollins*Religious*,
Part of HarperCollins*Publishers*,
77–85 Fulham Palace Road, London W6 8JB

First published in Great Britain
in 1992 by Marshall Pickering

1 3 5 7 9 10 8 6 4 2

A catalogue record for this book is
available from the British Library

ISBN 0 551 02585 9

Printed and bound in Great Britain by
HarperCollinsManufacturing Glasgow

Contents

Read this first – please

In this book we have tried to put together a collection of ideas that can be used with your youth group. This is not in any sense a definitive list – it is just a mixed selection of activities we have all employed and which have worked. We have tried to give them an evangelistic flavour in order to encourage your young people to reach out to their friends. All the activities have been road-tested – in places as diverse as Liverpool, Oxford, Surrey, Cleveland, Somerset, Lancashire, Bristol and Estonia!

In using the ideas in this book the important thing to remember is that you should always change and adapt the basic suggestions to your own particular situation.

This book of evangelistic ideas for youth groups is prompted by the fact that we are now well into the Decade of Evangelism. We hope that the ideas in this book will help you and your young people to reach out to those around you with greater confidence and enthusiasm.

We are today reaching out from a position of strength, because if you take all the denominations, you will find that in many areas of the country the Church has more young people attending its voluntary groups than any other organization. That is encouraging news. It should be not a reason for complacency but rather a cause to continue with renewed enthusiasm the good work that goes on all over the country.

PART 1
WHAT MAKES
EVANGELISM WORK?

What makes Evangelism work?

Churches everywhere must seek new ways of passing on the faith to the children and young people growing up in the congregation and the neighbourhood.

(Faith in the City, 6.114)

The word "evangelism" is one which has a host of connotations to a whole variety of people. Some Christians will describe themselves as evangelical; others will use different labels. Often evangelism is associated with street preachers and mass rallies. But the biblical perspective is that evangelism is to do with *every* Christian sharing his or her faith in both *word* and *action*. It is about passing on the Good News that God has revealed himself in Christ.

I recently came across a lovely story which well illustrates what evangelism is really about. The story revolves around Brother John. He was a monk who lived in a remote monastery in northern England. He was very happy in his job, and the special responsibilities he had in the kitchen kept him busy. However, one day a new Abbot was appointed. He proved to be rather strict, and insisted that every monk should take his turn in preaching. Brother John was rather disturbed by this because he did not like preaching sermons, since he could never think of anything to say. But the Abbot insisted that he should take his turn.

Eventually the Sunday arrived when Brother John was due to preach. The time came for the sermon and he ascended the pulpit steps. He was extremely nervous and had long been in a cold sweat. Leaning over the pulpit, he said to the congregation, "Have you any idea what I'm going to say this morning?" The reply came back, "No". "Well, neither have I", said Brother John, and he jumped down from the pulpit and ran into the Vestry.

The Abbot was furious and was hot on his heels. Giving him a good telling off, he insisted that on the next Sunday he was to deliver a proper sermon. The next Sunday came, and again Brother John nervously ascended into the pulpit. Looking down on the congregation, he said, "Have you any idea what I'm going to say this morning?" Seeking to encourage him, the congregation this time said "Yes." To which he replied, "Well then, there is no need for me to tell you!" and off he shot into the Vestry. The Abbot was red with fury and hotly pursued him, cornering him against the cupboards in the Vestry. "Next Sunday," he said, "you will preach a full and proper sermon, or there will be trouble."

Brother John knew that there was no way he could get out of his obligation this time. So Sunday came, and he ascended into the pulpit for the third time. He again asked the congregation, "Have you any idea what I'm going to say this morning?" This time the congregation were unsure what to say; some muttered "Yes" and some "No". Then Brother John said, "'Those who know tell those who don't know." At which point he again jumped down from the pulpit and raced into the Vestry. Meekly standing in the corner, he fearfully awaited the wrath of the Abbot. However, much to his surprise nothing happened, and for ten minutes he stood there hearing only chatter coming from the church. Eventually the Abbot did appear, but with a broad smile on his face. "That was the best sermon I have ever heard", he said. 'Those who know tell those who don't know' – brilliant! That is what evangelism is all about."

The best evangelism with a church youth group will be through the members' friendships at school or in the neighbourhood. In fact, if there is a group within a church who can and will share the Good News, it will often be the young people. When young people begin to realize the power and love of Christ in their lives, they are usually keen to tell their friends about it.

Taking Steps

Here are some simple steps which you can take to encourage your teenagers to share their faith.

1. *Good Teaching:* If your young people are encouraged and helped to understand clearly what it means to be a Christian and to live a Christian life, this will have a vital part to play. The Bible is inherently a dynamic and powerful book which expresses the wonder of what God can do for you and me – it is Good News. If your teenagers understand that it is Good News for them, then they will develop a concern to share it with others.

2. *The Holy Spirit:* Unless we allow God to use us and to empower us with his Holy Spirit we will be wasting our time. The occasions when we worship and have fellowship together must be times when we acknowledge the divine presence of God in our midst. We are called to honour him and to be open to him. The Holy Spirit is the power of God: he gives substance to our words and worship, and without him everything is dry and lifeless. When young people are aware of the fellowship of the Holy Spirit and of his power in their lives, nothing can hold them back from the job of sharing the faith.

3. *Outward Looking:* If your group just see themselves as a church club and are exclusive, then you need to shake them up and turn their consciousness inside out so that they are outward looking. Some groups become stagnant and eventually die simply because they want to remain a closed little group and are unwilling to invite others along. You need to give them an awareness of what is happening around them and to encourage them to see beyond their

group to the needs of others. How do you do that? By laying on events and occasions which are not just for them. You need to change their social attitudes.

4. *Communicating:* If someone were to ask you to explain what it means to be a Christian and how to become one, do you think you could clearly articulate it? Do you think your teenagers could? Quite a number of Christian teenagers have difficulty in explaining the faith because they are not used to talking about the Gospel. The more discussion you can stimulate in the group the better, because that will help to overcome the problem. It may also be helpful occasionally to do a session on explaining the Gospel to people, and then to encourage the young people in pairs to explain to each other how you become a Christian. If you can get them to talk naturally about the faith, then they will find it easier to talk to non-believers.

5. *Equipping the Saints:* Even many adult church-goers are ignorant about certain simple aspects of the faith, and they find it difficult to articulate an answer to basic questions. Listed below are the ten most common objections to Christianity made by young people. Equipping your young people to be able to answer some of these questions will help build their confidence in talking to others:

- How do you know that God exists?
- How can you trust the Bible?
- What about people who never hear the Gospel?
- Why does God allow suffering and evil in the world?
- Aren't all religions the same?
- Isn't faith just psychological?
- How do we know that Jesus rose from the dead?
- Do you have to go to church to be a Christian?
- Aren't all good people Christians?
- What about the bad record of the Church?

When it comes to evangelism among young people, who does the job best? The young people themselves! It is the teenagers who are the best evangelists and encouragers among their own age group. They are the ones who reach their friends at school, at college and in the local neighbourhood. So equipping them to reach out to others will be your most effective form of evangelism.

Evangelism is transformation

In his book *Christian Youth Work* Mark Ashton makes the very valid comment that with teenagers it is often appropriate to speak of a four-year conversion. It is very easy to obtain an emotional decision from a teenager, but evangelism is really about an inner transformation. This transformation is something that takes time to become rooted and grounded so that it affects a person's real beliefs, values and priorities. Rallies, dynamic talks and travelling God-shows alone are not sufficient to sustain a young person in a real transformation of his or her life. In fact, some church evangelistic events are mostly "hype" and are as shallow as advertisements for washing powder. Such events are judged to be successful if they persuade a large number of young people to make a decision to follow Christ, but the question is, how many of those youngsters are living out their decision a year or two later?

Many youth leaders will know of teenagers who became Christians and at first were very enthusiastic, but as time went on they dropped out of church and the youth group. Leaders may also know of some young people who were once very committed to and involved in the church and who in many ways showed the hallmarks of mature faith, and yet when they went off to university or college they simply drifted away. In an age where life is very complex and young people are under immense pressure in a multitude of areas, their faith in God cannot be permanent unless it is allowed to work its way through their psychological, emotional and existential development as human beings. The powerful thing about Christ's ministry is that he exposed his disciples to all the sin and suffering of life. He did not dodge the difficult issues or deliver a half-baked Gospel; their discipleship involved a lot of loneliness and suffering. He showed them that what they believed in was worth living for and dying for. He spent three years with them before they eventually realized the full impact of what they had seen and heard. It would be naïve of us to think that helping our young people to find faith and to grow in it is not a long-term process.

The people "on the edge"

The most effective evangelism will be done with those who are on the edge of church life, for they will have some sympathy with and understanding of the faith. It is extremely rare for someone to come in "completely cold", without having had some meaningful link with the body of believers. The fascinating thing is that Jesus' ministry was so often aimed at those who were on the edge. People such as tax collectors, prostitutes and soldiers were the ones who readily received the Kingdom of God when they saw genuine faith and love. Jesus consistently discovered the presence of God in the person on the perimeter. It was they who had a real understanding of the nature of the Good News and who exhibited a quality of discipleship not to be found among the comfortable and the well settled.

In our evangelism among teenagers we should have open-handed ministry, be prepared to give and share with those around us without wanting something back. Many people are hesitant in developing an interest in and a commitment to the faith because they feel that they are wanted only as pew-fillers. We must adopt a "give-away love" that sees each person as someone of value in their own right. We must be genuinely interested in them as people, not just as potential members of the youth group or the church.

Those on the edge will be attracted by a group in which trust and real friendship exist, in which there is a concern for social justice, and in which there is freedom and open-mindedness as well as direction and a clear Christian awareness.

As Richard Raines once said: "Christianity is like electricity: it cannot enter a person unless it can pass through!" So the onus is on us to give it away.

16

PART 2
TRAINING YOUNG PEOPLE IN EVANGELISM

A note to leaders

This seven-part training course will give your young people a good grounding in the principles and practice of evangelism among their peer groups.

Training is important. Jesus trained his disciples before he sent them off on missions to evangelize. Part of our job in making disciples is to train them in evangelism, helping them to be effective witnesses for Christ. We are all called to witness to the life we have received from Christ. Young people especially have their part to play. If it's channelled well, their witnessing can be exciting and fresh.

When faced with taking part in evangelism of any kind, most of us have a number of questions or hesitations. The seven sessions here respond to the questions we might well ask if we are seeking to engage in outreach of any kind. What is the Gospel? Why should I bother? What do I do? What about all the hard questions people ask?

Working through the activities here will certainly increase your young people's confidence and effectiveness in carrying out any evangelistic events, but it's good also to have a long-term view of your work with your youth group. This training will help to prepare them to be leaders themselves in the years ahead.

Our advice is that you use some of this material before launching any event. Otherwise there's a danger that the event will flounder through lack of confidence. Indeed, it might actually have the effect of putting the young people's friends off. Do remember, though, that we learn by doing, so the activities can also be used after outreach of some kind has taken place.

Each session includes an introduction for the leader in order that he/she can be clear about the importance of the activity. An aim and some objectives are given in all the sessions but 6 and 7, where the objectives are self-evident. The objectives are useful because they focus for the leader the purpose of the meeting – i.e. "This is what I'm going to achieve with the group when we meet."

The activities vary. You can judge their suitability for your group by working through them yourself beforehand. Sometimes you will find it necessary to adapt the material a little to the needs of your group.

Session 1

What is the Gospel?

Why explain the Gospel again? There are three good reasons for teaching the Gospel afresh to your group. First, it makes good pastoral sense; secondly, it encourages deeper commitment; and thirdly, it makes for more effective evangelism.

Its pastoral value

One of the great emphases in the New Testament is assurance, or being sure of the Gospel. The leaders and teachers of the early Christians encouraged and pastored God's people most frequently by reminding them of what God had done for them and how God really saw them. Whenever people heard the Gospel it was Good News for them. It never became old news, because whenever it was taught it refreshed and revitalized their faith.

Although we are concerned primarily with learning to share our faith with other people, you will find that in teaching the Gospel to your group you will help them to be stronger in their faith and more ready to answer for themselves many of the obvious insecurities of this time in their lives – e.g. "Am I really accepted?" "What should my aim in life be?"

It encourages commitment

Apart from the pastoral usefulness of teaching the Gospel afresh to your group, you will find that some might be ready to commit their lives to God in a fuller way. Some of your group might have become Christians when they were much younger; for them the Christian faith has been part and parcel of their growing up. We all need to respond to

God's love for us in new and deeper ways when we learn more about him. Sharing the Gospel should engender greater commitment from your group.

It makes for more effective evangelism

It's been said of Billy Graham that not only did he preach the Gospel effectively, but he was also a remarkably successful salesman before he became a full-time evangelist! If you know the Gospel clearly and in detail you are more able to "sell your product". It's very difficult to talk about something you know nothing about! The more we know, the better able we are to explain what we know to someone else.

Aim

To help the members of the group to be sure of the Gospel.

Objectives

1.   For the group to understand where the Gospel is from, what it does and who it is for.

2.   For each member to be able to explain very simply how they know the Gospel is true.

3.   To begin to understand how we should respond to the Gospel, not just in a once-and-for-all way but in a continual way throughout our lives.

Opening talk

A Bible study based on Romans 1:16: "For I am not ashamed of the Gospel: it is the power of God for salvation to everyone who has faith, to the Jew first and also to the Greek." Use the points below and expand on them as you feel you need to.

1.   The verse is clearly about the Gospel. It tells us of the Gospel's *origin* from God. It is therefore not something that we have made up in order to keep the Church going or to meet people's need for religion. We know it is from God because of

(i) the coming of Christ;

(ii) its power to change things that we can't change – i.e. our sin;

(iii) its progress through history.

2.   The verse tells us about the *Gospel's effect*: the Gospel is dynamic, it is "the power of God for salvation". Mention your own testimony – how your life has changed since you've been a Christian. Highlight what the Gospel does for us in our past (sins forgiven), here and now (the strength of the Holy Spirit) and in the future (the promise of eternal life).

3.   The verse tells us who the Gospel is for: "to everyone who has faith, Jew and Greek." God has no favourites; the Gospel is for all people of all ages. You could give examples of missionary organizations which work in other countries.

Discussion

Use these questions to reinforce the opening talk. The answers are in brackets.

1.   Who is the Gospel about? Mark 1:1. (Jesus Christ. It is not mere stories about the effect of religion on people.)

2.   What can happen to the Gospel? Galatians 1:17–19. (It can become corrupted. Therefore there is only one Gospel.)

3.   How did Paul receive the Gospel? Galatians 1:11–12. (By revelation.)

4.   What was Peter's error, and what does this tell you about the Gospel? Galatians 2:11–14. (He separated

himself from people for whom the Gospel was intended. Therefore the Gospel affects how we live.)

5. What happens as the Gospel is spread? Colossians 1:1–6. (It produces fruit, i.e. it is received by people.)

Plenary

After the discussion emphasize the following points, which will help the group to know that they can be sure that the Gospel is true:

1. Many documents other than the Bible refer to the appearing of Jesus Christ.

2. The Church today might abuse or misuse Gospel principles, but that doesn't mean that the Gospel has failed. There is a difference between what God intended and what people have done.

3. We each receive a revelation of the Gospel in different ways. The important question is not when or how you came to know Christ, but do you know him now?

4. Someone once said, "The only sign of being converted is present convertedness."

5. God promises to bless us when we share the Gospel – it will produce fruit.

A Gospel outline

Ask the group to help you to organize and structure a Gospel outline. Use some of the material from Session 5, but also ask group members to say what they believed and what they did when they became Christians. The outline should include the bare essentials of what a person needs to believe about God and what they need to do themselves in order to respond to the Gospel. John 3:16 could be used to facilitate this.

Session 2

What is evangelism?

Bishop Stephen Neill, a famous missionary historian, said, "If everything is mission then nothing is mission." The same can be said of evangelism, you might be in danger of missing the specifics. People need to be told that a "Gospel of righteousness has been revealed" (Romans 1:17). The question is, how do we go about telling them? We are not all called to be platform speakers! The Bible gives a spectrum of ways in which evangelism takes place, all leading to the same result: the sharing of the Good News of God's love. People then come to accept what Christ did for them when he gave his life on the cross. In the New Testament evangelism takes place in three distinct ways:

1.   Through an evangelist – i.e. someone with a gift of proclaiming God's Word, so that people respond to Christ in faith for the first time. E.g. Philip (Acts 8:26f.) and Timothy (2 Timothy 4:5; Ephesians 4:11).

2.   Through Christians gossiping the Gospel and sharing their story. E.g. the Samaritan woman in John 4; see also 1 Peter 3:15.

3.   Through the witness and distinctive life-style of Christian believers: "that men may see your good works and glorify God" (Matthew 5:16); "all men will know you are my disciples by the love you have for one another" (John 13:35).

Methods may differ and the context in which evangelism takes place may vary, but sharing God's Word in God's way will enhance its effectiveness no end!

The Session is intended to raise your group's awareness

26

of these three areas. You need to emphasize the fact that most Christians operate only in areas 2 and 3. Only a few are called to be evangelists.

Aim

To help the group to realize that they have a part to play in God's work of evangelism.

Objectives

1. To highlight the work of evangelists and to encourage any young people with particular gifts for evangelism.

2. To encourage the group to talk about their faith in an "everyday context".

3. To challenge the group to live with an awareness that their actions as well as their words influence people for Christ.

Activities

Here are some suggestions for activities which will fulfil the above objectives. Choose those which best fit the context of your group.

1. The group could interview an evangelist about his/her job. What does he/she hope to achieve? How does he/she go about achieving it?

2. The group could attend a Guest Service and afterwards discuss their thoughts and feelings about the occasion.

3. Start a support scheme for an organization involved in evangelism. Make it part of your regular programme.

4. Identify and encourage any within the group who have specific "up front" evangelistic gifts. After some training, enable them to take part in an outreach activity.

5. "Why I am a Christian?" Divide the group into small groups, each of which should make a list of ten answers to this question.

6. Hold a debate on any one of the subjects below. Ask a few people to argue in favour of the proposition and ask some others to argue against it. This activity will bring into sharp relief issues which are often discussed, and it will give your group members greater confidence in relating their faith to these issues.
(i) Is God's ideal for marriage desirable? Why?
(ii) Is capital punishment right today?
(iii) Should Christians go to war?
(iv) Do "TV evangelists" aid the Christian cause?

7. Do a short Bible study on the importance of personal conversations and one-to-one work in evangelism.
(i) Look up the following stories: John 4:27–30; 1:43–49; 1:39–42. For each passage:
  (a) Who are the people who are meeting?
  (b) What is the relationship between them?
  (c) How did one person encourage the other to seek Christ?
(ii) In a larger group use a large sheet of paper to draw a network of relationships just to highlight who each person in the group is in contact with.
(iii) Suggest a prayer triplet scheme to pray for a number of friends on a regular basis.

8. Ask the group to think of a Christian they know whom they respect and admire. Ask them to write down what it is about that person which draws their respect. Make a list of general or specific characteristics and draw attention to those (i.e. the majority) which are connected with life-style.

9. Divide the group into small groups and ask them to make a list of areas of school or college life where there is a need for distinctive Christian witness. For example: use of

language, attitude to work, tolerance, co-operation etc.

10. Using the following scriptures, answer the questions below: 1 Peter 2:11–12; John 13:35; Matthew 5:13–14.
(i) What is being asked for?
(ii) Why is such behaviour asked for?
(iii) How can we live out these principles in our daily lives?

Session 3
What is so important about evangelism?

"Why should I bother with evangelism?" is a question which even mature, older Christians ask. Evangelism can be tough, unrewarding and hard work. With little response, sometimes a natural reaction is to take the easy course and not bother.

This activity is centred around a Bible study based on 2 Corinthians 5. The epistle as a whole is particularly revealing about the great apostle Paul's humanity. In 4:7 he speaks of "treasure in jars of clay", while in 5:4 he speaks of groaning and being burdened by his earthly toil. It is from these situations that he gives many powerful motives for keeping going in evangelism. We will consider four of them.

Enthusiasm for evangelism and commitment to it are infectious. Youth leaders need to review their own personal commitment to the task, as young people will easily see the duplicity of encouraging one thing whilst not living it yourself. Leaders should acknowledge that, like the young people, they have things to learn about evangelism. We can often be marvellously encouraged and inspired by young people's commitment.

The motives for evangelism which Paul gives in 2 Corinthians 5 are outlined below. Familiarization with them is necessary, so it might be helpful to consult a commentary to fill out any point you are wanting to make. You can then adopt any of the options suggested under "Activities" below.

Motives for evangelism

1. *The judgement of Christ.* "For we must all appear before the judgement seat of Christ, that each one may receive what is due to him for the things done while in the body, whether good or bad" (2 Corinthians 5:10). In our presentation of the Gospel we should always major on the love of God in Christ, but a powerful incentive to evangelize is the realization that one day "we must all appear before the judgement seat". Paul was certainly inspired by the certainty of this fact. The necessity for judgement can be explained by reference to loving, good, truthful and unselfish deeds. If hateful, lying and selfish behaviour were not judged, then good behaviour would have no ultimate meaning. Christ commands that we "Go and make disciples" because the "end of the age" is approaching. God wants "all men to be saved" from the Day of Judgement.

2. *The love of Christ.* "For Christ's love compels us, because we are convinced that one died for all, and therefore all died" (2 Corinthians 5:14). Christ's death was slow, painful and humiliating. Because he loved us, he sacrificed himself on our behalf. Any selfless act deserves respect and admiration; Christ's death for us, the ultimate act of self-sacrifice, should compel us to be tireless in the work of evangelism. See also John 3:16, 13:1; Romans 5:8; 1 John 4:9–10.

3. *The power of Christ.* "Therefore if anyone is in Christ, he is a new creation; the old has gone, the new has come!" (2 Corinthians 5:17). All Christians know that Christ has changed them in a way that no one else could have done; something new has come into their lives. Paul is motivated to share the Gospel with people because Christ has the power to create new life by his Spirit.

4. *The death of Christ.* "God made him who had no sin to be sin for us so that in him we might become the

31

righteousness of God" (2 Corinthians 5:21). Christ's death for us means that we can be accepted into God's presence. Only by Christ's death could the hand of God and the hand of mankind join. Luther expressed this powerfully: "Jesus became the greatest liar, perjurer, thief, adulterer and murderer that mankind has ever known." Jesus became these things for us – if he had not done so the hands of God and man would have remained far apart. The cross both starts our Christian faith and motivates us to keep sharing it.

Aim

To increase the group's motivation for the tasks of evangelism.

Activities

1. Encourage an awareness of the fact that there will be a Day of Judgement. E.g. collect together a pile of newspapers and get the group to cut out all the stories about people who suffered the consequences of their actions.

2. Emphasize that when evangelism gets hard we need to keep going.

3. Provide an opportunity for recommitment to God's work of evangelism. E.g. show a video which demonstrates what can happen when someone shares their faith.
(i) Then present a talk based on the four motives for evangelism.
(ii) Use the following questions to stimulate a discussion. Let the group members do the talking – you should take a back seat!
    (a) What happens to people who ignore the Gospel?
    (b) Someone claims that God doesn't love them. Think about why they might be saying that and formulate a possible answer.

(c) "I've done too many wrong things – God can't accept my past!" How would you respond to this?

(d) Why did Jesus say from the cross, "Today you will be with me in Paradise"? (Apart from the thief's response, "Today" means the day on which Jesus died to open heaven to all believers.)

Session 4

What do I tell people?

Evangelism takes place not only through the formal proclamation of the Gospel but also through people sharing with others their personal testimony of God's work in their lives. In the Acts of the Apostles Paul shares his testimony on three different occasions. On each occasion his testimony contained three essential elements:

1. What I was before I became a Christian.

2. How I became a Christian.

3. What Jesus Christ has meant in my life.

There are many biblical examples of people sharing their faith on a one-to-one basis. One of the most instructive is Jesus' conversation with the Samaritan woman in John 4. After her encounter with Jesus she went back to her village, and "Many Samaritans from that city believed in him because of the woman's testimony, 'He told me all I ever did'" (John 4:39). In whichever context your youth group do their evangelism, it will be invaluable for them to know the basic principles of sharing their faith on a personal basis.

Aim

To increase the group members' confidence about sharing their testimony and to emphasize the importance of personal conversation about the Christian faith.

Objectives

1. To write out personal testimonies and to share them with other members of the group.

2. To see how Jesus evangelized in personal conversation.

Activities

1. Using the three distinct areas mentioned above, ask the group to write down their testimony, bearing in mind some of the following principles.

(i) In sharing "What I was before I was a Christian", encourage the group to realize that this can vary in content, although not in essence. Depending on who they are sharing their testimony with, they can select parts of their life which they feel might identify them with the person listening. For example, they might say, "I always used to go to church, but it didn't mean anything" if they are aware that the listener is a church-goer.

(ii) Whilst identification with the listener is important, one should not overdo this part of one's testimony. It would be a mistake to spell out in great detail a life of social and spiritual rebellion that makes a criminal seem tame, or to feel that you have to add to the truth because you have never done anything particularly wrong! There is plenty of scope for humour in explaining your past.

(iii) Point out that in speaking about "How I became a Christian" it isn't necessary to explain the Gospel in detail. In fact this might be a hindrance: it could feed people with answers they could use to keep their distance. It would be better to say, "I came to the point where I wanted to become a Christian and so committed my life to God in prayer", rather than say what was prayed. This can be explained later.

(iv) Encourage your young people to be positive, honest and accurate when they are explaining "What Jesus Christ has meant in my life". All can testify to sins forgiven, strengthening by the Holy Spirit and assurance of eternal life, but there might be specific areas of change, e.g. ceasing to use bad language, etc.

It's worth spending time with the group to get confident and convincing testimonies. Far from manipulating them, this encourages them to think about how they are being heard by people. It is sad when someone who has genuinely met with the Lord is unable to convey that to their friends because of shyness, lack of confidence or incoherent thought.

2.   A Bible Study based on Jesus' conversation with the woman at the well in John 4. This shows how Jesus evangelized through personal conversation. Using John 4:1–42, in small groups answer the following questions:

(i) How did Jesus make contact with the woman?

(ii) How did he arouse her curiosity?

(iii) What was the sore spot in the woman's life which he touched?

(iv) How did he avoid the diversion the woman made (vv. 19–20)?

(v) What are natural points of contact with friends where Christianity is talked about?

(vi) Write down 4 or more sentences which, if said, would arouse your friends' curiosity.

(vii) What are some of the things people hide from today – things which might well be a "sore spot" for them?

(viii) What are some of the "red herrings" which people mention in conversations about the Christian faith? How do we seek to avoid them?

(ix) Jesus brought the woman to a place of personal commitment. How would we know if one of our friends was ready to make that step? (Session 5 explains what to do if that is the case.)

Session 5

My friend wants to become a Christian!

The New Testament uses graphic images to distinguish Christians from non-Christians. For example, "light and darkness", "sheep and goats", "wheat and tares", "believers and pagans". Whilst there are grey areas of interpretation in the Christian faith, entering the faith from a position outside it is for many a definite, clear commitment. Young people especially respond to the call for decision. In view of this, it is all the more important that it happens well and is in no way forced or manipulated. This Session aims to help your group to be aware of the need for serious consideration by anyone seeking to become a Christian. We will also look at the necesary steps to take if someone decides to become a Christian. They will be aware that it might be preferable for a leader to guide this process, but they might well be involved themselves. In each event they will have the information to be aware of this process rather than be in ignorance of it. In brief, the aim of this Session is to bring about a more articulate and informed response to this process than the statement, "Oh, they've prayed the prayer now"!

Aim

To show what happens when someone is led to Christ in a prayer of commitment.

Objectives

1.   To formulate a suitable prayer of commitment.

2.   To be able to guide someone who is seeking commitment with suitable Scripture verses.

3. To consider Philip the evangelist in order to be aware of the importance and seriousness of the process of leading someone to Christ.

Activities

1. In small groups the young people consider the Scripture verses below and write down what needs to be admitted, what needs to be believed, what needs to be considered and what needs to be decided.

Admit: Romans 3:10; 1 John 3:4; Romans 6:23
Believe: Romans 5:8; Galatians 3:10; Mark 10:45
Consider: Matthew 6:24; Luke 14:25–35
Decide: John 1:12; Revelation 3:20; Hebrews 3:7–8

2. Using some of the concepts and thoughts above, ask each group to write a model or example prayer of commitment. The reason for doing this is to demonstrate that the content of prayers is significant – i.e. we need to say more than "Jesus, take me as I am"! This exercise also dispels the myth that writing prayers of commitment is the preserve of evangelists. Having written a prayer of their very own, the young people will be encouraged to use it. (N.B. for both 1. and 2. it's necessary to go over the received material.)

3. Explain that the role of introducing another person to Christ is an important one. The Bible provides Philip as an example we can follow and be encouraged by. Using the following points, elaborate on Philip's qualities in a short talk. Read Acts 8:25–40.

(i) He was in touch with God (v. 26). We need to be too, so that he can use us.

(ii) He showed sensitivity to the Spirit's promptings (v. 29). We need to let God guide us.

(iii) He was tactful and he listened (v. 30). We need to listen before we can guide.

(iv) He was well informed (v. 35). We need to be familiar with the Scriptures.

(v) He was direct and challenging (v. 30). We need to be the same, otherwise ignorance and apathy will continue.

Use the example of Philip to encourage the group to be the sort of Christians whom God uses to lead people to Christ.

4. Ask each member of the group how they were led to Christ, if they were in a position where they made a decision. Suggest literature, like *Journey into Life*, which they could give to their friends if they were wanting to make this step. Mention too that leaders are happy to help and guide their friends if this is appropriate. Finally, encourage them to pray that they will see their friends make decisions for Christ.

Apologetics (1)

The next two Sessions are concerned with the subject of apologetics. Young people will often be asked questions about the Christian faith: "How do you account for . . . ?" These two Sessions provide both information and activities to enable the members of your group to give four answers to each of the issues we are looking at. Ideally each answer should be understood and learnt not in order to be repeated verbatim should a question arise, but as a basis for further thought on the issue.

The biblical encouragement for us to be involved in apologetics comes from at least two sources:

1.   "Always be prepared to give a reason for the hope which is within you" (1 Peter 3:15). This speaks for itself.

2.   "Love the Lord your God with all your heart, soul, *mind* and strength." The first commandment requires us to think about God's purposes in the world. In other words, we should not be ostriches with our heads and minds in the sand: we should not try to avoid hard questions.

Two questions are looked at in each Session. Each question is examined in a different way. It is possible to change the methods if you are familiar with the material.

What about other religions? Aren't there many ways to God?
1.   Ask the group to make a list of the world religions they know. Then ask them to list some of their *common* characteristics. You may need to have available some books about other religions.

2.   In smaller groups the young people look up the

following Scripture verses and answer the questions. The answers are given in brackets.

(i) John 14:6. Does Jesus say that there are other ways to God? (No! Christianity is the only religion which makes exclusive claims.)

(ii) John 1:1–4. Jesus is the focus for Christianity. Is it a man-made idea or does it come from God? How do we know this? (The appearing of Christ supports the Christian belief in revelation over and above the views of other religions, which present humanly organized beliefs. In none of the other religions does someone claim to be God!)

(iii) Matthew 25:31–46. On what basis are people judged to be worthy of entering the kingdom of heaven? How do you think God will judge people of other religions if they haven't heard the Gospel? (Possibly a response to the Gospel can be judged by how others are treated.)

(iv) Look up the following verses with the group and make the following points to them. Here is how other religions are mentioned in the Bible:
Genesis 20: Abimelech was not a Jew, but God had real communication with him.
Exodus 2:15–22: God was at work amongst the Egyptians, and therefore he is at work amongst other religions.
Deuteronomy 7:1–6: Some of the practices of other religions are evil and harmful.

3. It is hoped that the group will be able to learn that:
(i) Christianity makes exclusive claims for itself.
(ii) Christianity is about revelation – God communicating himself to man, and not the other way round.
(iii) God knows the hearts of all people, and he therefore knows how they will respond.
(iv) God is at work amongst other religions; real communication takes place. But some of their practices are harmful.

I just don't believe in God anyway. He doesn't exist.
Using an OHP or a large piece of paper, hold a brainstorm session with the group to see what immediate answers they would have to this suggestion. You might well uncover some good answers; these would be worth emphasizing. Four strong answers would be:

1.   The appearing of Jesus Christ, his claims to be God, his resurrection and the continual life of the Church must all be considered.

2.   Scientists agree that there is order as well as diversity in the created world. It seems logical to at least ask the question, "Is there a Designer behind the good design?"

3.   How do we know what is ultimately good unless there is a God who is good? Atheism ultimately leads to a relative view of morality. It tells you the sequence of the alphabet – M–N–O–P–Q–R etc. – but it can't say we begin at A. Ethically, reason only gets us from one position to another; it doesn't say where we start.

4.   To say, "I don't believe in God" is a position of faith in itself – it is not a position of total certainty. The question can equally be put, "How do you know there isn't a God?" "I'm not sure if there is" (agnosticism) is on safe ground and is an easier position to put evidence to.

Session 7
Apologetics (2)

This Session follows on from Session 6.

Why is there so much suffering in the world? Doesn't that count against a belief in God?
Divide the group into four sub-groups. Ask each sub-goup to look at one of the points below and then to report back to the larger group.

1.   Contrast a Christian and a non-Christian in a position of suffering (either through sickness or natural disaster). For the non-Christian, imagine their situation and write a poem entitled "Why is this happening?" For the Christian, write a prayer beginning with the phrase, "Why is this happening, Lord?"
   This activity makes the point that suffering is actually as hard, if not harder, for the non-Christian to come to terms with as it is for the Christian.

2.   Provide the group with some literature from Christian Aid or Tear Fund and ask them to show how Christians are involved in helping others who are suffering in one part of the world. This activity makes the point that Christians are involved in reaching out with practical, compassionate help to those who are suffering.

3.   For each of these situations, ask the group to decide who is responsible – individuals, governments, groups of people, or God?
(i) Someone loses a leg in a car accident. The driver was over the legal alcohol limit.
(ii) A crop harvest fails in Ethiopia through lack of rain. No money is made available in the country to provide alternative food.

(iii) An earthquake causes massive homelessness in Bangladesh.

(iv) A 20-year-old lady has a few months to live. The doctors and nurses have no treatment to guarantee a recovery.

Other scenarios can be thought of. The point needs to be made that suffering can be caused by human (individual or corporate) negligence. As free agents, all suffering we experience doesn't argue against God's power and sovereignty, otherwise our freedom is limited.

4. Read Romans 8:18–38 and answer:
(i) What does Paul mean by "everything" (v. 28)?
(ii) What is the "good" which each of us is called to (vv. 28–29)?
(iii) What confidence do we have in the face of suffering (v. 31)?

This passage makes the point that God works through suffering; our sufferings are transitory and in no way hinder God's purpose of us being made like his Son one day in glory.

As each group reports back summarize visually and verbally the four points:

1. A suffering world is even harder to understand without God.

2. Christians always seem to be involved in relieving suffering.

3. Suffering can be the result of the freedom which God has given us, and therefore in those cases it is our responsibility.

4. Suffering can be used by God.

Does science disprove a belief in God?

This question is dealt with through a debate. One group speaks for, another speaks against. Prompt each side with these pointers in addition to their own thoughts.

For: Yes, science does disprove God's existence.
1.   Miracles are contrary to modern science. We don't believe in them; we either reinterpret them or ignore them.
2.   The theory of evolution suggests that the world wasn't created by God.

Against: No, science doesn't disprove God's existence.
1.   What does science aim to do? It answers only "How?" questions, not "Why?" questions.
2.   Science isn't against God. The world can be studied.
3.   Ignoring miracles because they do not fit in with science's preconceptions is letting science tell us how things are. If they happened, then we need to take them into account. The right question is, "Is there evidence?" not "Is it possible?"
4.   Science is concerned with finding an ordered description of the way things are. If there is a God, then to ignore him would be to fail in our understanding of reality and therefore to fail in the scientific task.

PART 3
PRE-EVANGELISM

Taking Aim 1:
Introduction

It's a truism to say, "Aim at nothing and you won't be disappointed"! But Christian youth groups and their leaders ought to consider planning for evangelism for a more fundamental reason. Why? Because we serve a God who has a Master Plan and a purpose for his world (Ephesians 1:9–10). This plan includes young people.

Now add to this St Paul's description of Christians as "God's fellow workers" (2 Corinthians 6:1), and the importance of planning becomes even clearer. It's not about us drawing up our own plan to save the universe, or even our little bit of it! It's about falling in step and joining in with what God is already doing.

The idea of a mission audit for churches has become popular recently. It gets a church:

- *Looking up* – to catch a fresh vision of God's overarching purposes.
- *Looking out* – to see the sort of people around – their needs, the opportunities to express God's love. Where is God at work? Where does he want to be at work?
- *Looking in* – to see to what extent the church is "fit and ready" to join in as God's fellow workers.
- *Looking for* – a realistic plan of action based on what they have seen.
- *Looking lively* – to take that action and assess its results.

What works for churches can work for youth groups too. "Taking Aim" can help you and your youth group to:

- encounter God afresh;
- see where he is at work in evangelism;
- evaluate your group's fitness to join in;

49

● plan, take and assess realistic action.

"Taking Aim" is a project about evangelism which could be included alongside the other aims of your group – fun, social, worship, nurture, etc. But it could also help you to see how evangelism can be a natural element in all you do together.

Taking Aim 2:
Looking up

Method

A Bible study to help leaders to focus on God's agenda for evangelism and on our part in it.

Equipment

Large sheets of paper, a jumbo marker, Bibles, songbooks.

Preparation

Prior reading of the passage. Give some thought to the worship.

Action

"Count your blessings!" It's a popular antidote for the blues! In fact it's a great exercise for Christians, blue or not. It's one that St Paul recommended to his friends at Ephesus, to help them "take a fresh aim" on God, themselves and his will! Only when leaders have taken aim themselves can they really help their youth group to do so too!

1.   *Talk about:* What has your experience of plans and planning been – on the receiving end or as one doing it? How do you feel about seeing God as a "Planner"?

2.   Read Ephesians 1:3–14.

3.   Together "count your blessings" as Christians from this passage. Call them out with the verse, jotting them on

a large sheet of paper divided into four. Head this first section "Blessings".

4.   In pairs hunt for verses which refer to or explain God's purpose or will. Share these and jot them down headed "God's eye view". This is the bigger picture in which *we* have a part to play!

5.   The little phrase, "for the praise of His glory" (vv. 12, 14) keeps recurring. It isn't just about worship with our lips, but how our lives and words and actions can draw others to praise God's glory and to know and love Him. In other words it's about evangelism! Discuss the motives for evangelism you find here and honestly assess how they compare with your own feelings.

6.   Together ask, "What resources for evangelism does this passage point to?" Jot them down headed "Resources".

7.   Together spend time worshipping God, allowing the truth of his blessings, purpose and resources to touch you afresh. Thank him for how all this can be true for you as leaders and for your youth group.

8.   Try to complete these sentences together:
To be "blessed in Christ" (v. 3) means . . . . . .
The purpose God has is . . . . . .
The resources God gives are . . . . . .

9.   Think about individually: How does it feel to be working with the great Planner? Is there anything I must now do from what I've learned?

Taking Aim 3:

Looking in and out

Aim

An outline to help leaders to look at their group and their opportunities, to plan and to set goals for action.

Content

The following material needs to be adapted to your own needs and time restraints. However, the basic outline should be retained, as it leads you through a reviewing process.

Please remember to commit the whole thing in individual prayer and pray together at every stage. Also, plan as we may, the Holy Spirit blows where he will!

Looking in

Sometimes we wish it wasn't the case, but starting from where you're at *is* the only place! What is your youth group like? How fit are you for evangelism?

1.   Read John 17:20–26. This is what Jesus prayed for his group just before his death. Note that he is praying that they will show to the world the same things about God that he showed while on earth. He prays that others will discover:

● the love of God (v. 26)
● the truth of God (v. 20)
● the living reality of God (v. 21)

– and all through coming into contact with them as a group of people. These three things can be a yard-stick to measure where you are at as a group.

2. Compile an honest profile of your group. Use these key headings:

● What we are (John 17:26).
● What we do (John 17:20).
● How God really figures in our group (John 17:21).

Be realistic about the good and the not-so-good. The following lists may help you:

What we are
Numbers, ages, boy/girl mix, group's name, schools, backgrounds, money, a group or a collection of individuals, image. When we meet, where we meet. Growing, shrinking, static, overstretched. Zany, boring, irrelevant, a riot, violent, exciting, attractively different, popular. Real, warm, credible, caring, compassionate, cold, unaware, accessible, a sanctuary. An extension of Sunday School, a club, a nurture group, outreach.

What we do
Games, outdoor pursuits, socials, Bible study, food, prayer, worship, arts and crafts, life skills. Open House, drama. Counselling, befriending, reaching out, wait for others to come, hit the streets, support, bail out, keep them off the streets, nurture, entertain, evangelize.

How God figures
Reality. "Oh no!", open to questions, unseen presence, Lord, alive, softly-softly, know about, know personally, we meet on church property, service, sacrifice, risk, faith, holiness, worship, evangelism, revelation.

Pause to thank God for your group – for its life and members.

3. Discuss together:
(i) How does what we *are* help/hinder people to encounter the *love* of God?
(ii) What is there in what we *do* that helps/hinders people

to encounter the truth of God?

(iii) In what ways do we *show* that God is alive and exciting to us?

Looking out

Jesus prayed the prayer in John 17 so that "the world" – people who don't yet know about him – would come to know him. Who in the world does God want to know about him through your group?

1. On a fresh sheet of paper, draw up a "target" of 3 concentric circles. Starting from the bull's eye, mark them "does", "could" and "might".

2. Discuss and jot down the individuals and groups to whom your group does/could/might show the love of God. Include as much as you know about them. For example:

Does – those in the group or on the fringe who are "just looking" and asking questions, and who are not yet Christians.

Could – those young people with whom a real link exists. To reach them will require stretching your faith, but God is giving opportunities. This group might include friends of members, a teenage confirmation group, the ones who hang around outside at a distance on club nights.

Might – well, you never know! This is in the "mountain moving" league. But dream for the future!

The "does" and "could" groups are the relevant ones. They represent those young people whom God wants your group to reach for him!

Looking for

This is who we are, what we do, the image of God we present. These are the people we do and could reach for God. In order to reach them, what are our strengths to be built on? What are the things which need to change, the gaps in our group life that need to be filled?

So, what steps do you need to take to achieve this? It might help to keep thinking about this in terms of what we are, what we do and how God figures. Some of this planning will be for you as leaders alone. Some will be in close consultation with the group, helping them to catch the same vision of evangelism you have and showing them how they can be a part of it. The rest of this book gives realistic ideas for training, enabling and events.

Perhaps at this stage you could ask the opinion of church leaders or others outside your group too.

Looking lively

Plans are fine. But it's action that you're after!

1. Be specific and realistic in what you plan. Who is responsible to do what by when? These headings may help:

| *What* | *How* | *When* | *Who* |
| we want to do | we can do it | we'll do it by | is doing what |

2. Set a time-scale.

3. Set aside time to evaluate the success of individual events. Periodically check your overall progress against your group profile and aims.

Prayer and prayer ideas

"The harvest is plentiful . . . Ask the Lord of the harvest to send out workers . . . Go!" (Luke 10). In these words Jesus ties together three elements: a vision of a ripe harvest of souls, prayer and evangelism. Notice the sequence: prayer is at the heart. "Ask . . .!" But do we?

If our evangelism among young people is to be effective we must follow this pattern, with prayer at the heart. By doing so we align ourselves with a vision of what is possible – the harvest – and draw on God's resources for the task. As St Augustine put it, "Without God we cannot. Without us he will not."

The rest of this part consists of ideas to get your group praying for their part in evangelism. The key factors are creating a sense of expectation that God will act, providing stimulating methods of praying, and encouraging young people to look for and thank God for answers to prayer.

Circles of prayer

Method

A check on how outward-looking you are in prayer.

Action

During a normal prayer slot in your evening programme plot the focus of the prayers said on a diagram, without your group knowing. Draw a series of concentric circles. Label the inner ring "Me", the next "Family", the next "Friends", the next "My school" etc. to include the world. As people pray, plot the prayer with a cross. At the end show the plot to your group. Discuss the distribution of the crosses. What does this say about our field of concern in general and our concern for evangelism in particular?

Prayer on paper

Method

Writing down prayer requests as you pray.

Action

This is a helpful way of praying in general. Firstly, it focuses the request in a tangible way, engaging brain before mouth! Secondly, "recording" a name or a one-word summary of a request can make real the faith of the pray-er and the others in the group. Thirdly, it helps the less eloquent. Also, it provides a check-list to measure answered prayer.

There are endless variations as to how this can be used. The only equipment needed is a big sheet of paper and a jumbo marker.

For example:

- If praying for an area, photocopy a map. As you pray, mark crosses on the map for the road, youth club, home, etc., you want to pray for.
- If praying for youngsters in the church, draw a silhouette of the building. As you pray, write their names round the edge with an arrow into the church, to represent your prayer that they will come in.
- If praying about inviting people to an evangelistic event, get a programme, posters, etc. Mark the names on paper. As you pray, move the invites, etc., onto the name and pray together.

The empty chair

Method

A visual aid in prayer to keep outreach on the agenda.

Action

When praying in small or large groups, include an empty chair to symbolize the person or group being prayed for – pray that the chair will be filled! This acts as a reminder and a stimulus to imagination as young people pray: what is this group or person like, interested in, etc.?

Huddle grace

Method

Relaxed physical contact in prayer to help build a sense of belonging.

Action

Group members gather in a circle with eyes closed. Each reaches in with a right hand to grab someone else's right hand. Repeat with left hands. Squashed together, say the words of the Grace: "May the grace of our Lord Jesus Christ, the love of God and the fellowship of the Holy Spirit be with us all. Amen." Now get out of that without letting go!

This is an ideal fun way to end a meeting. It can also draw outsiders into an activity and make people feel more relaxed about praying.

The prayer game

Method

Stimulating prayer using a simple board-game.

Action

Draw a series of squares to create a course round a "board" of thick paper. Mark each square with a prayer topic. Include several marked "Prayer". Throw a dice and pray for whatever topic is marked on the space landed on. Written prayers are prepared beforehand to be read by those who land on "Prayer" spaces. This game can be adapted for any emphasis, including prayer for evangelism.

Prayer stations

Method

Using several "prayer stations" for short, relevant input and prayer.

Action

This is adapting Spring Harvest's fast-moving debate idea for use with prayer. Prepare by selecting 4 evangelistic topics for prayer. Ask 4 members to research 1 each; they should be prepared to give 2 minutes of input ending with 3 specific prayer pointers. Make a prayer station for each topic – the stations are broomsticks with cards bearing the topics attached.

On the day, divide your group into 4 subgroups. Each sub-group is to move round the room to each prayer station. At each they hear the 2-minute input, and then they pray about the 3 pointers for 3 minutes. They then move on to the next station.

Prayer walk

Method

Small groups walking an area, praying for a specific need for those they encounter.

Action

This increasingly popular method of praying can really bring prayer alive and "deliver" prayer in a very immediate way! Agree to pray either for young people in general in a geographical area, or for an area of concern within a location – e.g. local schools, a hang-out place, etc. Prayer walks are especially effective before an evangelistic event.

After a time of worship and prayer together, move out in pre-arranged groups of 3 to pray as you walk. Pray silently as you walk or stop and "chat" in prayer. You don't need to close your eyes or throw yourself on your knees on the pavement! In fact, no one needs to be aware you are even praying. Meet up at an arranged time for coffee and feedback.

Variation

Encourage members to use walks through town, to school, etc. as opportunities to "prayer walk" as they go.

Hints and hazards

Send older Christians with younger ones. Be aware of the safety aspect: go in threes and not after dark.

Youth ministry prayer group

Method

Establishing a prayer support group for youth ministry in general and youth evangelism in particular.

Action

This is an effective way of releasing prayer, and it draws a wider range of people into youth work.

The key to the success of such a group is always to remember that your aim is to pray for young people and evangelism, not to merely chat about them. Agree on when you will meet and for how long. Emphasize the importance of private prayer between meetings.

The leader should plan ahead to have a clear outline of the meeting – what to pray for, who will give up-dates and information so that prayer is relevant, review answers to prayer. Keep the sections of input and prayer fairly short, and include a variety of topics, perhaps grouped around a central theme. It is also helpful to produce an outline sheet of the evening, with Bible verses and prayer headings. As the evening proceeds members can add more detailed information under each heading and use the sheet for their own prayers in between meetings. Give the members a copy of your youth group programme so that they can be praying each week for your events. Also, try using ways of praying which your youth group enjoy.

Hints and hazards

Be aware of the confidentiality of what is said in your youth group. Tell the young people that the youth ministry prayer group exists – it will amaze them! – but assure them of confidentiality, especially if parents are involved!

Prayer in small groups

Method

The use of small groups as a safe place for praying and sharing hopes for evangelism.

Action

Large groups of silent teenagers with down-cast eyes are the biggest turn-off to expectant and personal prayer about anything, let alone evangelism. Splitting into groups of 3 or so (2 is awkward) for a specific time with a specific prayer task can fill a room with the buzz of prayer. Share, then pray. The leader is the time-keeper, moving people on from sharing to praying, telling them there is 1 minute left.

Small groups work. Why? Because it's safe. In small groups it's OK to pray silently or out loud. It's OK to dare to voice a hope that my friend X will come to this event, or that I will have the courage to say what I have been doing on a Sunday, etc. Small groups can also revolutionize how people pray once back in the larger group again.

Prayer Triplets were one of the great spin-offs of Mission England: groups of 3 Christians meeting together regularly to pray for 9 non-Christian friends. Youth group members could either meet on their own during the week, or you could include a 10-minute slot in your evening meeting for your triplets to pray. A good time to do this could be before the main meeting begins, to avoid pressure on those who don't want to pray.

Echo prayers

Method

Using New Testament prayers and encouragements to evangelism as a basis for praying.

Action

Read the passage together as a group. Then get the members to read it on their own, looking for a phrase or word that really strikes them. How might it apply to someone they know, to an event or situation that is coming up?

Now use the passage as a basis for prayer. Turn individual phrase into prayers, substituting new names, etc. Or try rewriting the entire passage as a prayer for your group or situation today.

Try these passages:

John 17:20–26	1 Thessalonians 1:4–5
Acts 4:23–31	1 Thessalonians 3:12
Acts 9:10–19	2 Thessalonians 1:11–12
Ephesians 3:7–13	2 Thessalonians 3:1
Ephesians 3:14–21	1 Timothy 1:12
Colossians 1:9–14	Hebrews 13:20–21
Colossians 4:2–6	Revelation 7:9–12

Variations

Be on the look-out for written prayers from other sources to use and adapt. E.g. church service books, material for the Decade of Evangelism, *Prayers for Teenagers* (ed. Nick Aiken).

PART 4
THE PERFORMING ARTS

Introduction

There are a number of ways in which the arts can be used for evangelism, and how they are used will be dependent upon a group's circumstances, gifts and talents. One constant problem with the use of the arts, however, is that styles and tastes are always changing. Hip-Hop and Rap have become popular styles of music over the last five years, but by the time this book is published they may be on the way out. We need to know what is happening at street level so that we, as Christians, are not just following the trends but are involved at the forefront of the action.

There are three possible ways of using the performing and visual arts for evangelism in the youth group situation:

1. To evangelize non-Christians within the group.

2. To draw people into the group through a service or event at which they may be evangelized.

3. To take arts out from the group to where young people are and to evangelize there.

Over the last four years we have taken teams of young people out on faith-sharing trips into schools, youth groups and churches, using a variety of performing and visual arts to proclaim the Good News. So the examples, suggestions and ideas here in Part 4 are all based on practical experience with our young people.

We have used the term "workshop" to describe some of the sessions, as it is important that we should be concerned as much with the process as with the product of the exercise. The young people need to engage with the medium of evangelism as well as with the message, so that they can be comfortable and relaxed as they sing, act, perform mime, etc. They will be using gifts which God has given them, and they will also be developing gifts which have previously been dormant. Our role as youth leaders is to help our young people to develop, to encourage spontaneity and new ideas. This is so much more productive than saying, "I want you to do the sketch in the way that I saw Riding Lights do it."

Evangelism through the arts is not about getting the right formulas and routines; it should be centred on the Good News which we have discovered. Our aim must be to transmit the Gospel effectively through the arts.

If such evangelism is to have an impact (and, indeed, if it is to be worth doing at all), it must be a prayer-based activity. However good the idea, its effect will be negligible and short-lived unless the prayer preparation and support is there. We would like to encourage you to consider prayerfully each of the suggestions which we make and to establish prayer as the basis of all your evangelism.

Dance workshop 1

Dance workshop 1 is for beginners.

Aim

To explore movement as an expression of worship.

Preparation

Book the hall. Bear in mind that bare floors are better than carpeted ones.

Preparatory session

1. *Open with prayer.*

2. *Biblical basis:*
We worship God with our whole being.
David danced before the Lord (2 Samuel 6:14).
Our bodies are living sacrifices – worshipping God (Romans 2:1).

3. *Warm-up 1:* Everyone walks around the edge of the room, slowly at first and in the same direction. There is to be no physical contact as the group moves. Encourage the group to move faster gradually until they are practically running, but still without any contact. Thus the group moves quickly but in a controlled way, as they weave in and out.

   Perform the same exercise for a second time, one half of the group walking clockwise around the room and the other half walking anti-clockwise.

4. *Warm-up 2:* Each dancer finds a space in the hall. The purpose of this exercise is to explore the limits of a "box"

73

which surrounds each person. Encourage the dancers to reach up as high as they can to touch the upper limits of their box. They should reach out in each direction – left, right, diagonally and stretched out on the floor – to discover their box and to become comfortable in it.

Accompanied by music, the dancers now develop patterns of movement which use all dimensions of their boxes. Perhaps ask them to form pairs and to verbally and visually show each other around their respective boxes.

Ask the dancers, in their individual boxes, to form shapes which express various ideas, e.g. sorrow, happiness, joy, Christmas, God's love, etc. They form each shape after a count of four.

Divide the group into four equal teams and put each team in a corner of the room. Each person is given a number. When a person's number is called they have to run into the centre of the room, jump in the air and land in a position which expresses anger, fury, dismay, jealousy, fear, etc. For example, number one is called, and all four number ones run and jump accordingly. This can provide a lovely mixture of spontaneous expression.

Main session

Give each team a short chorus or a simple Bible study to look at (plus pens and paper). Their task is to break the chorus or Bible study down into its different aspects or scenes and then to find positions which express these. Here is an example of a chorus which has been broken down in this way:

Great / is the Lord / and most worthy / of praise, /
The city / of our God, / the holy place . . . .

When this has been done, the positions need to be strung together and performed while the chorus is sung or the Bible verse is read. You will be amazed at the variety of interpretation and expression.

The next stage is to move on to an actual dance. It is a good idea to start with a simple routine and to build from there. Do not be afraid to use modern dance movements if you feel you need to.

Explore movement together, try things out, invent. If it doesn't work, have a laugh about it and do it all in the love of Christ (Colossians 3:12–14), always ensuring that the group members feel that their contribution is valuable.

Dance workshop 2

Dance workshop 2 is for those who have some experience of dance.

Preparatory session

1. *Open with prayer.*

2. *Biblical basis:* You may need to do this in some depth. Here are some of the issues which may come up: What is it appropriate to wear? (The sexuality of dance.) Does dance in worship have to be "airy-fairy" or can it have punch, impact and men?!

3. *Warm-up:* Ask everyone to do their usual warm-up exercises and routines. While they are doing these watch for movements which you may be able to incorporate in dances. Some of the most basic ballet exercises are very simple and yet have great potential.

Main session

- The workshop will need to be participative, with dialogue and exchange of ideas, so ensure that everyone knows that their opinions are valid and worthwhile.
- It is a good idea to begin with the Lord's Prayer, which contains themes such as forgiveness, freedom, trust, etc. Get the group to explore the words and themes and to express them in movement. Alternatively they could choose positions that suggest what the prayer is saying. Another good prayer to use is the Anglican Confession: "Almighty God, our heavenly Father, we have sinned against you . . ." This helps the group to get into the idea

76

of giving themselves to God rather than just dancing for the sake of entertainment.

- Move on to a song or a Bible passage that you would like to be portrayed through dance. The group members should discuss it, sharing their ideas and feelings. Experiment, and don't be afraid if someone says, "Patrick Swayze's step sequence from *Dirty Dancing* would go really well here"!
- When you have finished, over a cup of tea explain the arrangements for using the dance in worship. Plan another meeting.

School Assembly 1

School assemblies are great opportunities for demonstrating and proclaiming the Good News. Often assemblies carry the reputation of being dull and irrelevant, and sometimes even the Christian one can hardly be described as being Good News! It is therefore important to make the most of the opportunities given to us for this kind of work. Many of the workshops here in Part 4 are highly visual, attractive and dramatic ways of conveying the truth of who Jesus is and what he has done: why not use some of these ideas in a school assembly?

Action

1.   The following are all activities which our youth groups have done in school assemblies:

- Lead worship
- Sing Christian songs
- Give a talk
- Give testimonies
- Interviews
- Drama
- Mime
- Dance
- Rap
- Poetry

2.   Many young people would find it incredibly hard to stand up in front of their school mates and proclaim their faith, and we must be sensitive to this. You may find, however, as we did, that other young people are more than willing to make a stand, and we need to encourage them.

3.   In order to facilitate this kind of evangelism, youth workers need to have good relationships with the staff of their local schools. Often the young people will have to negotiate with teachers and do a fair bit of the arranging themselves.

School Assembly 2

School Assembly 2 is very different to Assembly 1. This uses professional Christian artists, who come and sing, perform sketches and mimes, etc. This can be a highly effective form of evangelism, especially if it is linked to visits into individual lessons, or to an evening concert or to a youth group special event.

Action

1. A certain amount of negotiation will be involved. You will have to discuss suitable dates with the school and the artists, and the school authorities will want to take up references and talk to the artist concerned. Most schools are very supportive and encourage Christian input, so be sensitive and follow their advice and recommendations.

2. Plan follow-up events and ensure that loads of publicity material for them is available. E.g., if there are going to be lunchtime discussion groups, put up posters stating when and where they will be happening. Alternatively, announce the details in the school notices.

Drama workshops

Young people's drama can be exciting, lively, creative and challenging – or it can be inaudible, stilted, boring and unedifying. Some questions that need to be asked are:
1. Why are we doing this?
2. Who are we doing it for?
3. What is it going to achieve?
The type of workshop to be held will be determined by how the above questions are answered. For example:

A home drama evening
1. Why are we doing this? To challenge our group with, e.g., Jesus' teaching on forgiveness.
2. Who are we doing it for? – Our group.
3. What is it going to achieve? It will help those who find it difficult to accept and experience God's forgiveness.

Street theatre in a shopping precinct
1. Why are we doing this? Because Jesus tells us to go and make disciples.
2. Who are we doing it for? The non-Christians who hang out in the precinct.
3. What is it going to achieve? It will demonstrate the Gospel message in a style that young people can relate to.

It is instantly clear that both these drama workshops are evangelistic, but they are also very different. Some groups could do both, while for others only one might be wholly appropriate. The material is desgined to be adapted to suit.

Home drama evening

Method

Hold a drama evening in a friendly setting that encourages intimacy. If the church hall is the only space that you have, try dimming the lights, adding colour or music, etc.

Warm-up

Use a number of warm-up games and exercises to loosen people up and to help them become relaxed and comfortable. (For suggestions see *Youthbuilders* and *Big Ideas for Small Youth Groups* (both published by HarperCollins.)

Main session

1. Sit together and share out copies of a chosen Bible passage. It is good to have it typed out so that no one has to struggle with finding chapter and verse.

2. Read the passage. There are several possibilities at this stage:
(i) Get people to take on the different characters in the passage. E.g., looking at John 8:1–11, the characters might be Jesus, the woman, the disciples, the Pharisees, the scribes, the temple guards, onlookers, etc. Look at how they might have reacted – their moods and actions – then act these out.
(ii) Do a TV news report on the biblical passage. A reporter interviews some of the characters. This helps the group to develop the characters more thoroughly and to anticipate their moods, responses and actions.
(iii) Concentrate on one character and act out how he or

she felt during the incident. This could be done using two
characters in conflict. Form two groups, one to represent
each character, and get them to act out responses as the
narrator reads the story.

Variations

There are lots of good books on Christian drama that will
give you loads of ideas and resources, but it can be just as
much fun to experiment and develop ideas yourselves.

Debrief

After the drama has been performed, it is beneficial to
gather together to debrief. Talk about:

- What actually happened?
- Who did what?
- How did they feel about Jesus? Has the drama changed
  their feelings about him?
- Was there a character whom they particularly identified
  with? Why?

Close with prayer.

Street theatre

Good street theatre gathers a crowd and holds them while the message is put over. Therefore

- Street theatre needs to be visual.
- It needs to be audible.
- It needs to be dynamic.
- It needs to be short.
- It needs to be rehearsed.
- It needs to be rehearsed *again*.

Hints

- Short, simple sketches are best. Jesus taught in parables – stories that often made only one point and left people to think it out.
- Air-horns, whistles, musical instruments, activities, bright clothes/costumes, etc. can all help to draw a crowd. Be different!
- Why not try sketches using simple deaf-and-dumb sign language to music? This can be highly effective if done well.
- If sketches and simple dance routines can be put to music, record it and play it on a ghetto-blaster so that the crowd can hear.
- Props should be simple – remember that you will probably have to carry them. They can be highly effective. Chairs, deck-chairs, step-ladders and dustbins all have great potential.

Action

1. Gather those who are interested. Spend more time in prayer.
2. Discuss who the evangelism is for and what you want to say through it.
3. What are the things that interest the young people? What are the relevant issues in their lives? Link these to Jesus' teaching and to Gospel themes.
4. What can we present in our street theatre, bearing in mind the answers to the questions above?
5. Brainstorm on these questions; look at resources, books and the group's own ideas.
6. Try out a few ideas and see how they work.

● Practise your street theatre and then perform it. Afterwards review how it went, so that the next time it will be better.

A praise march

With the March for Jesus and the Make Way marches over the last few years, youth praise marches have suddenly become a major item on the agenda for evangelism. They are a great opportunity for young people to get out onto the streets to witness to their own age group.

What is a praise march?

At its simplest it is a mobile service on the streets, using song, prayer, chants and responsive shouts, all proclaiming the Good News message. These are usually accompanied by banners, balloons, hats and streamers – in fact anything that adds life and colour, contributing to a feeling of celebration and carnival.

Action

1. Sell the idea to the young people. Organizing the march will involve a lot of work, so there is a need for enthusiasm and a willingess to work hard for a big project.

2. Divide up all the tasks that have to be done, and allocate teams to the different areas of responsibility.
(i) *Publicity*. Visiting other groups, using local radio, newspapers and TV, etc.
(ii) *Technical equipment*. A lorry for the music group, plus amplifying equipment, a generator, etc.
(iii) *Prayer base*. Evangelism is grounded on prayer. Form prayer triplets (give them another name, perhaps) to intercede for the march. Share together as a group what prayers have been answered, what progress has been made and what still needs to be prayed for.

(iv) *Music*. The musicians will have to get together, choose the music to be performed and practise it.

(v) *Literature*. You will need to produce prayer up-dates, word-sheets for the march (containing the shouts, songs and set prayers) and evangelistic literature to be handed out on the day.

(vi) *Follow-up*. What are you going to do with those who respond or show an interest? E.g. a special service, nurture groups, "Just Looking" groups, etc.

(vii) *Plan the route*. You will need to do this in liaison with the local police, whom we have found to be really helpful.

(viii) *Impact*. Balloons, banners, dance, street theatre, etc. – all these can be incorporated for added impact.

(ix) *Budgeting*. You will need to find sources of finance and plan your expenditure. One of the best ways of raising money for the project is to encourage your young people to contribute tithes towards it.

3. The teams may need to draw on adult help, advice and resources; the adults should be ready to assist the young people, but they should not try to do the work for them. The teams will probably need to meet every 2 or 3 weeks, and the team leaders every month.

4. Let the event evolve; the young people's ideas may be different from yours, but it is their evangelism. So let things take their course.

Variations

There are a number of alternatives if you cannot organize a lorry and a band. Use taped music or a walking group playing brass/wind instruments. Guitars, unfortunately, are not very audible over long distances, but they can accompany the singing in the march.

Resources

- "Make Way" tapes and music are available from Christian bookshops.
- March for Jesus (P.O. Box 39, Sunbury on Thames, Middx., TW16 6PP) have information available and will be happy to help.

Rap workshop

With the Rap, Hip-Hop and Garage scene being so popular at the moment, why not use these mediums evangelistically? (Rap is speaking in time to a beat originating from the streets of the USA. It often expresses concern about social justice, deprivation and life in the ghetto. In the commercial form its lyrical content is much the same as that of most contemporary music.)

Equipment

- You can do a simple rap using just a voice or voices.
- Rap over an instrumental dance track with a good beat and a speed suitable for your rap. (Most dance tracks have their speeds in BPM (beats per minute) on the sleeve.)
- Each person speaking will need a microphone for amplification.
- You could use a drummer instead of a dance track.
- Use keyboards and/or sequencers. (Sequencers internally record layers of sound and variations.) This way you can produce the whole thing yourself, but this is very difficult without expert help and expensive equipment.

What to do

1. Rap is about rhythm. Your young people will be able to demonstrate where and how to put the emphasis on words to give the feel.

2. There are a number of raps about on the Christian scene, e.g. "The Nathan Rap", "The Pharisee Rap" and "The Gospel Rap". It is good to write your own, and it's

fun as well. What your rap will be used for determines the content: e.g. a Bible story, an everyday situation or a rap specifically for evangelism, containing the Gospel message. Here is an example:

Eve's story

There was Eve in the garden one day,
Along came Satan with something to say.
He said, "Look at that apple – it's big and it's bright;
While Adam's away, why not just take a bite?
Do you want to live in this garden with me?
Eat this apple and you'll be like God, don't you see?"
Eve said, "Wow, it's got to be good!
Thanks for the chance, but I think that I should
Check it with the boss, 'cause he really said 'No'."
"Well, you got to be quick, 'cause I've got to go.
Anyway, he doesn't really care about you,
Else why did he leave the apple to grow?
It looks so good, quite a tasty treat,
Yet he hasn't allowed you and Adam to eat
Just one bite, one little delight.
You'll soon know it'll be all right."
Eve reached for the tree, she took one bite,
And a silent scream echoed into the night . . .

3. Practise it! It will take quite a bit of work to get the voices, movement and timing right. There is nothing worse than a rap no one can hear, so if you are using microphones there will need to be one per person. They need to be hand-held and held close and at the right angle when being used.

4. There is the potential to develop rap in complexity, using multiple voices, scratching, mixing, sound effects and talking. It is good to get the basics right before moving on.

5. Where to use it:
- In youth services.
- On the streets.
- At school assemblies.
- At a Megado.

A youth newspaper

Young people love drawing cartoons and writing creatively, so why not put these talents to good use in a youth newspaper? But before you can decide when and how large the first print-run should be, here are some questions to answer.

Questions

What is it for?
- Is it to be a theological treatise on the third chapter of Leviticus with cartoon summaries?
- Is it to be a glorified programme card, with forthcoming events and reviews about what has been done?
- Is it to be a creative expression of what being a Christian and a young person is like, and will it address issues that non-Christian young people can identify with?

Who is it for?
- Is it for the youth group?
- Is it for the parents and church members?
- Is it for the young people who never go to church?

Who decides what goes in it?
- Them?
- Us?
- The minister?
- Someone else?
- Where does the editorial power lie, and who carries the can when someone is upset by an article?

How will it be paid for?
- Subscription?
- Subsidies?
- Youth group funds?

How will it be produced?
- For small runs, the cheapest way is to photocopy it; for larger runs, printing is better.
- Should articles be typed or handwritten? Would desktop publishing and computer graphics be useful? How about Clip-Art books? What size should the newspaper be? What about its layout style? How many pages should it have?

Hints

Before deciding to produce a youth newspaper you will need to work through many of the above questions. If you intend it to be evangelistic, how will that affect the content? Above all, remember that it is *hard work*!

Circus skills

Method

There are a growing number of theatre groups and workshops that teach circus skills to young people and youth groups. Your local Association of Youth Clubs or your County Youth Officer will probably be able to give you details of any in your area. Why not have a fun time learning how to ride a unicycle or walk on stilts? The possibilities are endless, and remember that you will also be witnessing to those who come to lead the workshop!

Action

1. When the youth group are comfortable with the activities, take them and their new skills out onto the streets. They can use these as they give out leaflets for an event (e.g. a megado, a concert or a late-night youth service) or as they hand out evangelistic material. Circus skills can also be used to encourage young people to watch a street theatre or listen to a rap, etc.

2. *Some skills you could use:*

Clowns/face-painting	Stilt-walking
Juggling	Acrobatics
Unicycling	Fire-eating!

Hints

Although the activities are fairly safe, do check your youth group insurance before you start, in case there are any accidents.

Radio

With increasing numbers of local and community radio stations being set up, there is ample opportunity for Christian young people to get involved in this area. Here are some practical ways for young people to get started. Although they are not directly evangelistic, they create opportunities for evangelism by raising awareness, promoting issues and putting Christian young people on the front line.

Ideas for programmes

1. *Interviews*. If you are involved as a youth group in a project such as a schools mission, a youth service, supporting a Third World church, a fast for a charity, etc., then ask the local radio station if the group can talk about it, mentioning why they are involved in such a project and who will benefit from it. We have found that our local radio station is always helpful and willing to give air time and support to positive young people's projects.

2. *News items and diary dates*
Keep your local radio stations well informed about events and developments in your youth group. This helps to build up a good relationship. Remember that you are a witness to those working at the radio station as well as those they broadcast to.

3. *"Pause For Thought"*

Most radio stations run a "God Slot". Often these are only 1 minute long and out of peak time, but they are still well listened to. Why not ask those responsible (sometimes the radio station will ask local church leaders to organize the "God Slot") if your young people can present a "Pause for Thought" programme for a week?

Your young people will need some coaching in how to speak on radio and several trial runs before going to the studio to record. All they have to do then is encourage their friends to listen in. In inviting their friends to listen, the young people are publicizing the fact that they are Christians, even if the friends never even listen to the broadcast.

4. *Youth programme.*
Persuade your local radio station to run a regular youth programme, with young people choosing the music, addressing topics and current issues, interviewing, etc. Include a regular Christian input as part of this.

"Radio Cracker"
In 1991 the "Radio Cracker" project involved setting up Christian radio stations run by the young people themselves for the three weeks up until Christmas. To find out more about this contact OASIS, 22 Tower Bridge Road, London SE1 4TR.

Hospital radio
Why not approach your local hospital radio station and get your young people involved there as a stepping-stone to and a preparation for involvement in local radio.

Music workshop 1

Aim

To learn to play Christian worship songs together.

Action

1.   Choose a time, a date and a venue.

2.   Inform all the young people.

3.   Obtain copies of music.

4.   Borrow a tape player and some worship tapes containing songs to be learnt.

5.   Borrow an amplifier, etc.

On the day

1.   Set up the equipment and tune up.

2.   Open the session with a time of prayer together.

3.   Play through a song until everyone has got the hang of it.

4.   Things that need to be worked out: How to begin? How to end? What happens in between?

5.   Practise the arrangement decided above.

6.   Move on to another song.

7.   For example, your arrangement for "Hosanna" might look like this:
   Intro: drums × 4 beats.
   Verse 1: "Hosanna" – all.

Verse 2: "Glory" – all.
Verse 3: "Glory" – drums and vocals only.
Verse 4: "Hosanna" – all.
Finish: repeat from "Be exalted . . .", slowing, finish all together.

How to use the music

A music workshop may be a valuable evangelistic springboard in two ways. Firstly, it can be a means of encouraging and challenging the faith of those involved, leading the young people into a deeper commitment both to God and to sharing that faith in the music they produce. Secondly, the workshop can be the beginning of an exploration of different ways in which music may be used to reach young people. Here are some ways that we have used in the last three years with our young people.

1.   *Youth services.* These are an excellent form of outreach, involving lively praise and worship, fun talks, an informal style and atmosphere and lots of youth participation. It is best to hold these events late in the morning or in the evening, as teenagers don't like getting up early!

2.   *School assemblies.* If the musicians can get together at school, a few lively Christian songs will make a change from the usual dull assembly. This will be even more effective if the young people are given the opportunity to talk about what the songs mean to them.
  Remember:

● This should be done prayerfully.
● Check that the young people have permission to do it.
● If they need equipment, ensure that they can obtain it. They may need transport for it too.
● Don't force your young people into this; it's tough enough just being a Christian at school.

97

3.   *Scouts and Guides*. Scout and Guide camps sometimes generate opportunities to provide worship. A young people's music group can be very effective in these situations, as the youngsters hear about God from people their own age and see the Christian faith demonstrated in a way which is relevant to them.

4.   *Visiting other youth groups and churches*. Your youth group may be invited to bring their music to youth services in other churches or to evangelistic evenings run by other youth groups. Perhaps other groups are trying to explore the use of music and would be encouraged by a visit from your group.

Music workshop 2

Aim

To learn to play Christian and secular music together.

Action

As workshop 1, except using different types of music.

On the day

1. Tune up!

2. Practise a few songs (mixing the Christian and the secular), practise them again, and decide that it sounds horrible; everyone then jams together and make a terrible noise; then call the group to silence – especially the drummer! Then after a deep breath, run through the songs again.

3. Over the weeks of practise, begin to build up a repertoire of songs. Use modern, well-known music and try to combine different beats, rhythms and sounds.

How to use the music

1. Concerts.

2. Youth clubs.

3. Busking and street music.

A Megado

Aim

To put on a Megado – a multi-media, evangelistic, inter-group, participative youth event.

Information

A Megado (you might think of a different name) is where a number of youth groups get together to put on an evening of entertainment and evangelism, using home-grown talent. The ingredients are dependent on the participating groups' skills and abilities.

Action

1.   Sound out the idea on your young people and see if they think it would work. Maybe ask other youth leaders in the area to sound out their young people's feelings and comments as well.

2.   If the idea has youth support, choose a date and a venue. If the event might become a regular feature, then a "neutral" venue has advantages; or each of the participating youth groups could have a turn at being host. If the event is to be a "one off", find out which venue the young people feel is the most attractive.

3.   Send letters, posters and information to other youth groups. You could even send along a couple of young people to sell the idea (personal contact is always the most effectiv way). The purpose is not only to talk about the idea but to discuss possibilities and how all the different groups may participate. Find one young person in each

church to be a representative.

4.   Contact all of the youth groups to discover what acts, performers, rock groups, dramas, comedians, etc., are preparing to take part. Begin preparing your own youth contributions. If the acts look a little thin, you may need to draw in an adult band or speaker; this is only optional, however.

5.   Distribute publicity to all the churches, schools, youth clubs, etc., in the areas. Check out the venue. How does the lighting system work? Will you need to bring your own amplification? What about refreshments? etc., etc.

On the day

You will need to have enough helpers to cover all of the tasks which need to be done:

● Admissions.
● Lighting and PA systems.
● Drinks and refreshments.
● Host-compere.
● Stage crew and roadies.
● Counsellors and follow-up team.

After the event

Review, analyze and decide how to do it better next time.

Rave in the Nave

It's 8 p.m., and the darkened church is full of young people. A hush descends and a voice comes over the PA: "This is the Eight o'Clock Slot. Welcome to Theo's Praise Plus!"

Beethoven's Pastoral Symphony starts over the PA and a back projector puts the image of a paradise garden onto a huge white banner hanging off one of the beams. The music fades, coloured spotlights dance around the church and come to rest at the front as three young people begin to rap out "Eve's Story".

As the rap ends, the church falls into darkness and a voice explains what sin is and how, through Jesus, we can be forgiven. The ultraviolet lights suddenly come on and light up two enormous crosses as the people are urged to confess their sin to God.

The band strikes up with "Jesus Christ is Lord" and everyone is up on the pews, dancing and singing. Another Praise Plus is in full swing. During the evening there are dances, testimonies, a time for spiritual gifts, an evangelistic address, lively praise and a Taizé chant. There are lights, smoke, OHP picture-prayers, back-projected images and responsive shouts. It all ends with a big "Amen!" after the last chorus.

Youth services can be *for* young people – they do not have to be stepping-stones into the church's "main worship". Why not use youth services in a culturally relevant way for young people?

Ingredients

Music group
Taped music
PA system
OHP
Slide projector
Video projector

Pin spots
Spotlights
Minimoog
Ultraviolet lights
Smoke machine
Banners

Ultraviolet paint
Dramas
Raps
Dances
Mimes

Why do it?

We tried this kind of service at 6.30 p.m. without really asking anyone's permission. The teenagers said that if church was like this, they would have no problems in inviting all their friends. The adults, however, went up the wall! As a consequence, we tried it out later at 8 p.m. Sure enough, the teenagers were much more willing to come to this kind of service than to a traditional youth service, especially those with no previous church connection.

Dangers!

Don't let the service become more like a concert than an act of worship. The following are essential elements:

1. The real presence of the Holy Spirit.
2. Base the event on prayer.
3. Participation.
4. A liturgical format. Liturgy doesn't necessarily mean old-fashioned words (but these can, of course, be included if you wish). The important thing is to be inventive and to do everything to glorify God.

Other performing arts ideas

Christian concerts

The subject of putting on a Christian concert is covered in Part 8, so all I can say is, give it a go!

Busking

Christian music on the streets . . . Try it and see!

Street processions

1.   A quiet version of a Praise March. E.g. a Good Friday procession, using a huge cross. Give out hot cross buns and leaflets.

2.   A poverty procession, with everyone barefoot and dressed in rags, giving out appropriate literature.

3.   A "convict" procession, with "jailers" (representing greed, lust, envy, etc).

4.   An anti-abortion procession and vigil.

Remember that you will need:
Prayer support and church backing.
Police permission.
Plenty of press coverage.

Poetry

There are some great Christian poets about – people who can convey the Gospel in the words and pictures of today's culture. There may be one lurking in your youth group, so why not have a creative writing evening to draw him/her out? You could use the poems in a Megado or a school assembly.

A mime workshop

This is similar to dance and drama. It is best to try it and see how it goes. White gloves give it a professional touch!

Video

There are a number of evangelistic Christian videos around which you could use. Alternatively, why not hire a video camera and create your own blockbuster to show at the next Megado?

Summary of Part 4

Idea	Resources	Preparation time	Group size
Dance workshop 1	Worship tape	2–4 weeks	Any
Dance workshop 2	Worship tape	2–4 weeks	Any
School assembly 1	The Youth Group	2–4 weeks	Any
School assembly 2	A professional	3 months	Any
Drama workshop 2		Days	Any
Street theatre	Airhorns, whistles, etc.	2–4 weeks	Medium+
Praise march	P.A.	6 months	Large
Rap workshop		Days	Medium
Youth newspaper	Photocopier/Printer	2–4 weeks	Medium+
Circus skills		3–6 months	Any
Radio		3+ months	Any
Music workshop 1		Days	Medium+
Music workshop 2		Days	Medium+
Megado		3 months	Any
Rave in the Nave	Sound and light equipment	2–4 weeks	Medium
Christian concerts		6–12 months	Any
Busking		2–4 weeks	Medium
Street processions	Banners, music	2 months	Medium/large
Poetry		Days	Any
Mime workshop		2–4 weeks	Any
Video		2 weeks	Any

PART 5
EVANGELISM THROUGH SMALL GROUP ACTIVITIES

Introduction

The Bible commands us to go and share the Good News,
but how do we go about it? All of us have at some point
made an attempt to share our faith with a friend, only to
come away feeling as though we were a bit like an elephant
on ice and wondering if our friend would ever speak to us
again!

How do you reach those who are closest to you? How
can you share your faith with your neighbour or best
friend? How can you possibly start up a conversation that
will introduce Christianity without seeming to be a bore?

All of us have wondered about these questions and have
struggled to find answers. In this chapter I would like to
share with you some ideas that have worked for us or for
other youth groups that we know about, where young
people have attempted to reach out to those whom they
care so much about.

All of these ideas will involve your group working
together. They will also find it easier to share their faith
from within the security of a group.

None of the following ideas is fool-proof, and will only
work if prayer, energy and enthusiasm are evident in the
lives of those taking part. However, all of the ideas have
been and are being used. Every one of them has worked
and can work for your group.

Most of the ideas involve some cost, and so it might be
worth approaching your church leadership to see if they are
prepared to give you a specific evangelism budget to help
you on your way.

Barbecue and games evening

Method

Hold a barbecue and games evening at a leader's house with the aim of showing that Christians can have fun and introducing some of the youth group members' non-Christian friends (e.g. school-friends and neighbours) to their Christian friends.

Numbers

Ideal numbers would be between 12 and 18. It is important that there are quite a few invited guests as well as a good number of youth group members. If they are greatly outnumbered, the guests may feel threatened.

Equipment

You will need a number of games that will help people to mix together. Some suggestions: badminton, french cricket, boules, football, twister, etc. A large barbecue with fire-lighters, charcoal and matches.

Preparation

Ask each of your youth group members to bring something towards the food, e.g. one person should bring a salad, another a sweet, another some baps, etc. Each member should also bring enough meat for him/herself and a guest.

Set some of the games up in the garden before anybody arrives so that there is something to do as soon as people start turning up.

Cost

Very little cost is involved. You will need to have a back-up supply of soft drinks, sausages, meat burgers and vegetable burgers. The main outlay will be the charcoal.

Action

1. The main activities will be eating and chatting. If some people don't want to take part in the games, try to involve them in the cooking so that everybody feels a part of the evening.

2. As always with an activity that involves food, people will soon relax and feel at home. End the evening with coffee and a short chat about why you meet as a group, outlining your future programme.

3. It is very important to have something specific happening the next week, so that you can invite the guests to it as a group. Your youth group members got them to come to the barbecue and games evening – you have to do all you can to make sure that they come again the next week.

Hints

If you pick a night during the week you are less likely to be competing with parties, etc. Offer lifts home afterwards – it's a good opportunity to chat and parents will appreciate it!

Evaluation

You will know that the evening has been a success if the guests attend the following week's meeting. However, make sure that you contact the members of your group who brought friends to see what the reaction was.

Beach/lake party

Method

This is a great fun evening out, and it will attract a good number of people. Take your group, plus friends, to a beach or lake, organize games and music and have a party. You could add to this a barbecue which makes any party a success.

Numbers

The more people you take, the more fun the evening will be. Aim to take at least 30 if you can. Those youth groups which struggle with low numbers will have to pull out all the stops, but it will be worth it. One way of getting the numbers up is to invite another local church youth group to come along with you. The last time we did this event we took 60, and we still could have taken more.

Equipment

All the equipment you need to play football, volley-ball, rounders, tennis, etc., plus garden spades and barbecue equipment.

Preparation

1. Beg or borrow a mini-bus if at all possible. Other churches and youth clubs and local councils often hire them out quite cheaply. Or ask your Diocesan Youth Officer where you can get one from.

2. If you are going to have a barbecue you will need enough equipment to match the number of young people

attending. Rotary Clubs are quite good at lending this sort of equipment.

3.   Getting permission to have a bonfire/barbecue on the beach/lakeside is very important. Contact the local council by letter and get written permission if possible. Otherwise find a place where you know that it is allowed.

4.   One carful of people should go in advance and build a fire from driftwood.

Cost

If you take about 30 young people £3 per head should cover petrol and food.

Action

Enjoy playing games and eating food. If you are on a beach, fighting the tide is fun. Light the fire as the evening draws in, and as everybody begins to relax after a busy time end with a short epilogue. Always finish the evening with an invitation to your next event.

Bonfire Night party

Method

There are certain events during each year which are superb opportunities for evangelism. Bonfire Night is perhaps one of the easiest to use, and it always draws a good crowd.

Arrange a Bonfire Night party as near to 5th November as possible, making sure that you don't clash with any main event that your town or village might put on. Advertize the event in the local schools and at all the local churches in plenty of time, so that people will plan to come to your evening.

Number

This event can be as large or as small as you want to make it. We have found, however, that you need at least 20 to make it fun.

Equipment

Make sure that you take every safety precaution that you can. You will need at hand:

- Buckets of water (at last 3 is recommended).
- A hose which is attached to a tap and ready to be turned on.
- A safety rope to section off the display area.
- Good strong stakes to nail certain types of fireworks to.
- A first aid kit readily available, with one person in charge of it.
- Some form of outside lighting if possible.

You will also need:
- Plenty of wood to burn
- A good selection of fireworks with at least three "big" ones.
- A willing host who doesn't mind having his/her grass flattened!
- Paper plates and cups and plastic cutlery.

Preparation

1. This event will need either specific personal invites or very good general all-round advertising. Numbered tickets are always a good way of keeping track of how many will turn up.

2. Get your youth group to collect wood and other burnable objects and to build a good fire. Helpers will also be needed to cook soup, jacket potatoes and any other food that you want to provide.

3. Rope off the fireworks area before anybody arrives, and make sure that all fireworks are handed in to you before letting any off.

Cost

This depends entirely on what you are going to provide during the evening. If you work on an average of 25–30 people coming, then £2 each should cover soup, potatoes, sausages and beans and still leave about £35 available for fireworks. Selling cans of drink can also help to subsidize this sort of evening.

Action

1. Light the fire about five minutes before the start so that a good blaze is just beginning to happen as people arrive. Allow people time to chat and mix before serving the food.

2. After all the food has been served start the firework

display, allowing each firework to finish before lighting another (it's all too easy to run out in five minutes).

3.   When the display is over provide coffee or tea, and then give an epilogue, perhaps using the evening activities as illustrations. Always end the evening with an invitation to your next youth meeting, preferably with an actual printed/ photocopied invitation.

Ventures and camps

Method

Take your group to serve on a venture holiday with Crusaders, Scripture Union, CYFA Pathfinder Ventures or any other similar organization.

This is an area of evangelism that is so often overlooked. All year you will have been feeding and nurturing your group, and this gives them an excellent opportunity to give back some of the things that they have received.

This is an opportunity not to be missed. Those young people who go will be sharing their faith non-stop for a week and will come back with a new excitement about evangelism which can do nothing but put new life into your group.

Most ventures will only take helpers aged 16 and upwards.

Numbers

Unlimited. There are plenty of ventures and camps throughout the summer.

Preparation

Teach your young people about serving others and working in a team!

Cost

Usually leaders pay the same as the children, so this makes it a very expensive business. The average cost is approximately £90. However, grants are available from each of the different organizations. You could also ask your church leaders for financial help.

Hints

Go yourself! If you are enthusiastic about the holiday, this enthusiasm will flow over into your group.

Variation

Encourage your young people to bring friends with them on the holiday.

Evaluation

The great value of the holiday will be self-evident when the young people return!

Confirmation groups

Method

Confirmation is often seen as something young people do when they reach the age of about 14, and having "signed on" in the Church, they don't feel the need to come again, for a variety of reasons.

With this is mind, the suggestion is that the youth leaders, along with the youth group, run the Confirmation course, which will include a weekend or a week away. Your vicar, of course, should be invited in on a number of occasions so that he can have some input into the course.

Numbers

A maximum of 12 in a group.

Equipment

Confirmation course which has already been prepared. There are plenty of such courses available.

Preparation

1.   You will need the total support of your group in order to run this sort of venture. They will have to be prepared to pay for their own weekend/week away and to give up time each week to attend the Confirmation course with all of those taking part in it. Therefore careful planning will be needed with members of your group, making sure that they are prepared for the commitment.

2.   Pick your course carefully and plan a good fun weekend/week away in the middle of it.

3.   Advertise the course through as many channels as possible – at church, in the schools, in the youth group, etc.

4.   Personal invites from your group will help to attract many more young people.

Cost

It is possible to run a course *and* go away for a good weekend for approximately £50 per person. However, if you extend this to a week away the cost goes up to approximately £90.

Action

1.   Set up 10 weekly meetings with a weekend/week away in the middle of the course. Run it as you would a Christian Basics course. During the weekend/week away present the teaching about what it was that Jesus came to do (i.e. central Gospel teaching).

2.   Arrange for each member of your youth group to adopt a course candidate. Make it the member's responsibility to check that the candidate turns up each week.

3.   Make sure that you have a good teaching programme for your time away. It should allow each of the candidates to think for him/herself about Christianity without any pressures from home.

4.   Look forward to your youth group expanding as candidates join it at the end of the course!

Hints

For your time away it is best to go to a place where they arrange all the activities for you. This saves you a great deal of work and allows you to concentrate on the teaching. You might want to use Nick Aiken's book *Being Confirmed* which is especially written for young people.

"Just looking" evenings

Method

These events can be done in two ways. The first way is to hold an open evening during which a panel of mature Christians are asked questions relating to their faith. The second way is to form a discussion group to which your young people can invite their friends. This group could meet on several occasions.

Both of these methods of evangelism involve your young people in doing the hard work of bringing friends along, and both give you, the leader, the slightly easier job of sharing your faith and knowledge.

Numbers

For the panel evening you can have any number of people you like. However, if you have more than 20 people some of them won't get to ask any questions.

The discussion should not number more than 12 – i.e. 6 Christians and 6 friends.

Equipment

Time and energy.

Preparation

For the panel evening

1. Your youth group members must have some say about who is going to be on the panel. These people need to be approached in plenty of time and asked if they would be prepared to take part. A four-member panel gives plenty

of scope for a question being answerd by someone!

2. Make posters and advertise the event in all the schools which your group members attend. Encourge personal invitations and contact all those who have come to events before, asking if they would like to come to this one.

3. Plan the evening very carefully. Sunday night after church is often a good time; if they attend the evening service your guests will have plenty of ideas for questions.

4. Challenge your group members to bring along at least one friend each, or, better still, encourage them to invite a group of friends. There is safety in numbers and the response might be better.

For the discussion group

1. The invitations will need to be on a far more personal level and the numbers attending will be much smaller, but the quality of commitment afterwards will be greater.

2. Set up 5 meetings which will last a maximum of an hour each, and pick a suitable time in the week to have them. A time which has proved to be reasonably successful is 4.30–5.30 p.m. after school.

3. Plan each meeting and be well prepared with visual aids and fun things to do so that the group stays together throughout the 5 weeks.

4. Here is a suggested programme:
    Week 1: Jesus – did he exist, and if he did, who was he?
    Week 2: What did he come to do?
    Week 3: Is Christianity the Truth?
    Week 4: What's it like being a Christian?
    Week 5: The Church – what is it?

5. Begin each meeting with warm-up games and aim to create an atmosphere of warmth and friendship.

6. End session with coffee and a "feedback sheet" like the one below, so that you know you are not rushing ahead of your guests.

Feedback sheet

Please give this feedback sheet to
at the end of the session.
　Please tick the appropriate boxes. (Leave the sheet blank if you have nothing to say.)

I found this week's session
☐　Interesting/good fun
☐　OK
☐　Not very good because _____
_____
_____

☐　I would like the following questions answered ____
_____
_____

☐　I would like a private chat over a cup of coffee
Name _____

Action

For the panel evening

1. Provide drinks for people as they arrive and create an informal, chatty atmosphere.

2. Begin with some warm-up games which will break down a few barriers and encourage the questions to flow.

3. Ask the panel a few prepared questions and then invite questions from the young people present. If there are any

questions that cannot be answered ensure that you, as a leader, make a note of who asked them, and follow them up afterwards.

4.   End with coffee and an invitation to your next social and serious meetings.

For the discussion group

1.   Meet in someone's home and spend some time getting to know each of the guests. Make sure that you have their name, address and telephone number so that you can follow them up afterwards.

2.   Run each session in a light question-and-answer way that involves everybody. Always end with coffee and chat. Making friends with the guests is part of sharing our faith with them.

3.   Meet separately with each of the young people who have brought their friends along and spend time praying for the next session.

Door-to-door

Method

Take your group on a series of door-to-door visiting trips during which they will be able to share something of their faith.

Visiting part or all of a leader's road is perhaps the easiest way to start this sort of venture, because it gives you a place to go from and a place to return to which is close at hand.

Numbers

Unlimited.

Equipment

You will need something to give away at each of the houses you call at. Here are some suggestions.

- Cards inviting people to come along to a church service. These should include details of all the services your church offers.
- Cards inviting young people to come along to your youth group, with some details of your next few meetings.
- A parish magazine.

Preparation

1. This sort of activity will need some very careful preparation.

2. No one should go out visiting on their own or when it is dark – both of these things are dangerous and can scare

older people. Visiting should be done in twos, and there should be a leader within shouting distances at all times, just in case anybody needs any help. Leaders should also make sure that they are doing the visiting with the young people – leading by example is always the best way of making others enthusiastic.

3.   Inform your worship leaders of what you are doing so that they can make a special effort to welcome newcomers during the weeks following the visiting.

4.   Your group will need to be told the sort of things that they can and can't say.

Do's

Their main objective should be to share something of what is going on in the church and to invite people to come and join them in worshipping God on a Sunday.

- They should try to show that the church has life in it and that it is interested in reaching out to people.
- They should share something of their own faith, should the opportunity arise.
- They should promise to return another time if they are asked a question they can't answer. They should always make a note of the question and the name of the person asking it.
- They should always leave something with the people they visit, such as a parish magazine.

Don'ts:

- They should not promise a visit from the Minister (he/she might not be too pleased to have 50 extra visits to make the week before Christmas!)
- They should not try to answer questions they know nothing about.
- They should not enter into arguments about different styles of worship! They should always remember that

they are there to share their faith in Jesus and not to answer for the church.

5.   Finally, plan how many houses each pair should try to visit, and set a time at which all are to return to the leader's house.

Cost

The cost of the special invitation cards and the parish magazines.

Action

1.   Meet for prayer in the leader's house before anybody does any visiting. Go out knocking on doors in pairs and return at the set time, or before.

2.   Have a cup of coffee and chat about the evening's activity. Share with each other about the sort of visits you had and the type of response people gave you.

3.   Make a note of any follow-up visits that might be needed, and then end the evening with prayer.

4.   Each of your youth group members will now have the responsibility of looking out for people they visited who might come to church.

Evaluation

Often people will respond to a personal invitation to come to church, and special note needs to be made of the success of the visiting. Repeats of this event, if it proves to work in bringing people along to church, should happen fairly quickly, so that you keep the momentum going.

An alcohol-free bar

Aims

To set up and run an alcohol-free bar in your church hall or in a similar building. The evangelistic opportunities with this sort of thing are endless, but it does need commitment from both the youth group and the leaders.

The basic aims should be to reach out to those who don't come near your church for one reason or another, and to provide a meeting-place for them.

In setting up a non-alcoholic bar you will attract a good number from local schools, because you are doing something different. Once they are through the doors you have a captive audience for whatever you would like to put on.

The running of the bar will provide your group with the opportunity to speak to their friends about why they are doing it and who is running it. However, it need not end there. Invitations to singers and bands to come and perform will attract many more people, and the musicians will be putting over your message for you!

Numbers

Unlimited.

Equipment

- Plastic glasses (they are safe and cheap).
- A bar: either ask someone in the congregation to make one or make one as a group, keeping in mind that it will need to be moved when not in use.
- Pub games: a dartboard, a pool/snooker table, table

football, skittles and any other games you can provide cheaply.
● Chairs and tables.
● A stereo cassette player with a good selection of tapes.

Preparation

1. Decide how long you are going to run the bar for. A trial period of, say, 3–4 months gives you the opportunity to stop the bar if it doesn't work (very unlikely), but more important than that, it gives your group the opportunity to back out if they find the commitment too much. A good time to start a trial period is over the school summer holidays.

2. A decision will need to be taken about the age of the people you are going to allow in. 14/15–18 is a good age range, and the sort of age at which many young people are keen to find something to go to on a Friday night.

3. Opening hours will also need to be decided. These should be realistic: 8–11 p.m. is a good guideline to work with.

4. A list of non-alcoholic drinks will need to be drawn up, cocktails will need to be named and posters will need to be made. These should be as colourful and as professional as possible. Prices will also have to be decided on. Of the groups that are running this sort of bar at the moment, 50p seems to be the highest priced drink.

5. The more advertising you can do, the better this sort of project will be. Colourful posters put up in all the local churches and schools will attract a good number of people. It only takes about 7 or 8 people to set up and run a bar, but you can entertain up to about 80 easily.

6. Finally, give your bar a name! Names such as "The King's Arms", "The Vine" and "The Harvester" have been used in the past.

129

!! ONLY 45p !!

THE KING'S ARMS

COCKTAILS

Pina Colada

Sunrise

New!

OPENING June 7th

THE KING'S ARMS

AN ALCOHOL-FREE BAR

FRIDAY NIGHTS
8pm – 11:15pm

THE CENTRE, CHURCH LANE

14 years → UP

COCKTAILS · SNOOKER · POOL · MUSIC · DARTS · GARDEN

FRIDAY NIGHTS

THE

KING'S ARMS

Alcohol-Free

BAR

8 PM – 11:15 PM

The Centre , Church Lane

14 YEARS UP .

131

Cost

You will need the backing of your church, and so it is best to seek this before you start to do any advertising. Present a proposal to your church leaders and ask if they would be prepared to underwrite the initial financial outlay.

The bar itself should be self-financing, although a float of, say, £100 is needed to buy all the necessary equipment and to set things in motion properly.

Action

1.   Sell drinks, crisps, peanuts and sweets. Chat to all those who come to your bar. Play snooker and darts with them and show them that Christians are fun.

2.   Invite special guests such as Christian singers and groups. Hold *karaoke* evenings and competition evenings. Make your bar the place to be on a Friday evening, and then through your posters, your friendship and your talk, share your faith with all those who come.

3.   Always make sure that each table has a programme of your other events on display.

Hints

Adults always need to be present in case of any trouble. One adult to every 10 teenagers provides good cover.

Evaluation

Evaluate how the bar is going after three months, and if necessary close it until the next summer, or open it just once a month during term time.

This venture will take time and effort but the rewards can be enormous.

(Special thanks to St Mark's, Colney Heath, and to the SMYF Group for their help.)

Parents' and friends' evening

Aims

In our groups we often have young people who have either only one Christian parent or parents who will have very little contact with the Church. The aim of this evening is to provide an opportunity for each of the young people to communicate their faith to their family (either through a sketch or through talking about it openly), doing this with the security of working within the youth group. An evening like this also provides youth leaders with the opportunity to meet parents and chat to them.

Invite the parents/friends to a meal at your church hall which is cooked and served by the youth group.

Numbers

The numbers for this event will depend on how many are in the group. However, 20 guests should be the maximum, so that the leaders have the opportunity of meeting all of the parents.

Equipment

Cutlery, crockery, pots, pans, table-cloths, napkins, place cards, menu cards, music and any other item you can think of that will make this evening special.

Preparation

1. Make or print good-quality invitation cards and send them to all those you want to invite.

2. Organize some sketches (there are some very good

Christian drama books available – these will give you plenty of ideas). Plan very carefully. The more professional you make the evening, the more people will listen to what is being said.

3. Plan your menu so that not everything needs to be cooked at the last minute. Cooking some of the food the week before and freezing it will take pressure off the evening.

Cost

Parents won't mind paying for an evening like this. A meal with an evening's entertainment for £3 per head is very good value! A mere £3 shouldn't stop anyone coming.

Action

1. Have some people separated out as waiters and waitresses for the evening; they should serve drinks as the guests arrive. There will be plenty of chat to start with because of the nature of the evening.

2. Nominate one of the group to give thanks and then serve the meal promptly. Allow conversation to flow naturally between the guests so that those who attend the church services mix with those who don't.

3. As soon as the coffee is served start the entertainment. This should consist of sketches intermingled with thought provokers and should be rounded off with a short epilogue from one of the leaders.

4. As always, have something in which your group will be involved to invite people to, such as the next family church service.

Hints

If possible it is good to have some of the leaders sitting at the tables so that they can mix with the guests.

A party

Method

One of the activities which will always attract a good number of young people is a party. So hold a party for your group and their friends and arrange either for a good disc jockey to help out or for a Christian group to come and play.

Numbers

This will depend on where you hold the party. If there are 10 in your youth group, then you should aim at getting 80 friends to come along (Christian and non-Christian).

Equipment

Drinks, nibbles, music and a good atmosphere.

Preparation

As you probably won't know many of the guests who will be coming, it is best to give out tickets for this sort of event. Personal invitations to a fun evening are all that is needed. However, the guests should be told that there will be a Christian slot in the evening.

Cost

This will depend on the scale of the party. To hire a disco can be expensive, but it helps make a good evening, especially if the disc jockey is a Christian.

If the party is held in a hall, then it is perfectly acceptable to sell cans of drink, which helps to cover costs. A budget of 60p per head is a good guideline.

Action

Party, party, party! Encourage everyone to have a good time. Let the guests see that Christians are fun people to be with.

End the evening with a short epilogue from one of your group leaders, making sure that there is an invitation to another event. Handing out invitations to your next meeting is a good way of getting people to come along.

Hints

Have at least 1 leader to every 10 youngsters so that there are plenty of adults around, should there be any trouble.

Open house

Method

A regular slot in the week when a leader's house is open to group members and their friends. They can drop in, drink coffee, chat etc.

Numbers

As many as the leader's house can take.

Equipment

A house, coffee and tea.

Cost

This is costly to a leader in terms of time and effort, but youngsters do appreciate having an Open House to go to.

Action

Just providing unpressurized physical and emotional space for teenagers is not to be underestimated. Agree a regular time and day for a home to be open for young people to drop round. Open House isn't the leader "entertaining". In fact, get on with what you're doing! Open House gives your group members a space to bring their friends to – a place with an unthreatening, warm Christian atmosphere. Aim to treat the teenagers as young adults. Let them make the most of the opportunity to chat, whinge about the week, play records, etc. Once in a while drop in something gently Christian – e.g. a video or a discussion. You'll be amazed at who comes and how easily you just get chatting.

It will be easy to invite someone who has been to Open House to come to one of the regular youth group meeetings at the same venue.

Sunrise Easter Morning

Method

An early morning service followed by a "bring 'n' share" breakfast.

Numbers

10–15.

Equipment

A quiet location where you can see the dawn. Song-books, a guitar, a home, drinks and food.

Preparation

Find out when the dawn is – look it up in a newspaper. Group members should invite their friends. You will need musicians, someone to lead the prayers and someone to do a Scripture reading.

Action

1.   Getting up early can be a struggle, but also an exciting challenge! Many churches have a Holy Communion service at sunrise, but this can exclude unconfirmed teenagers and those on the edge of faith. A simple service (remember that it's early!) consisting of worship songs, a reading of the Resurrection story and prayer can be very powerful in such an unusual setting.

2. Here is a suggested outline:

Words of introduction: "Christ is risen!"
"He is risen indeed, Alleluia!"

Choruses: e.g. "Majesty", "Jesus Christ is risen today!"

Reading: Matthew 28:1–10. Then a time of quiet – perhaps give a question or verse to ponder over.

Chorus: e.g. "Led like a lamb to the slaughter."

Prayers: for the world, for your town, for yourselves, and a special Easter prayer.

Chorus: e.g. "Thine be the glory!"

3. Follow the service with a bring 'n' share breakfast at a nearby house. The menu? Eggs and left-over hot cross buns – what else?!

Hints and hazards

Plan to arrive before sunrise, so that it happens as you are worshipping. Since it will be very early in the morning, keep the service short. Watch out for the English weather. Have a Plan B, i.e. to meet in someone's lounge.

Variations

Any early morning can lend itself to a really different way of seeing the world and being open to God.

Graffiti wall

Method

Inviting young people on the street to contribute to a "graffiti wall" by writing their views on various topics.

Equipment

Lining paper, aerosol paint, jumbo markers, masking tape, invitations or evangelistic booklets.

Preparation

People need to feel comfortable and able to talk about their faith. A brief training session is a must. If you are going to have music or drama, it should be rehearsed.

Action

This activity not only gets people thinking, it can get them talking too!

1. On a wall or window in a prominent part of town, tape up a large area of lining paper. Get the owner's permission first!

2. In the centre of the paper write an incomplete slogan in spray-paint, e.g. "Christmas is . . ."

3. Invite passing teenagers to complete the slogan on different parts of the paper, using thick marker pens.

4. This provides a really natural conversation starter, i.e. "Why did you finish the slogan with those words?" etc.

5. Street music or drama helps to draw people's attention.

Have a supply of booklets to give to people to take away, if this is appropriate. You could also include invitations to a concert or a church carol service, etc., in the booklets.

Hints and hazards

Be sensitive to the area you live in, as people may think you are advocating graffiti. Get a splash in the local press in order to get the opposite message across! Talk to the local police. Make sure your markers don't go through the paper. Be prepared for some abusive comments!

Variations

- Here are some other slogans you could use:
  "Easter is . . ."
  "It's a Good Friday because . . ."
  "In AD 2000 I'll be . . ."
- You could do this activity indoors as a conversation starter.

The Duke of Edinburgh Awards Scheme

This Scheme is designed to draw on young people's energy and enthusiasm through a challenging programme of activities. It makes an ideal basis for the activities part of a church youth group programme.

Numbers

Any number. For expeditions you will need groups of at least 3.

Equipment

The activities do require equipment, but this can be borrowed from your local Youth Service stores at a very reasonable cost.

Preparation

Participants and leaders will require training for certain activities. If your group registers under your local County Council as the "Operations Authority", you will have to adhere to the Council's policy of qualifications. However, this does mean access to qualified personnel and resources. Also, contacts for various physical and service activities need to be made. A church is an ideal resource for such contacts.

Cost

Minimal, if you plan well and use volunteers. There will be some expenses for the use of equipment, travel, etc., so a costed per head charge should be made for each level of award.

Action

There are three levels of award: bronze, silver and gold. Each award is divided into four sections, the details of which are to be found in a comprehensive Handbook. The sections are as below:

1. *Skills:* Sustained interest and attainment of a reasonable degree of skill in one of a variety of areas.

2. *Physical activity:* Assessed participation in organized physical recreation and achievement of individual progress.

3. *Expedition:* A planned expedition on foot or by canoe, etc.

4. *Service:* Training in and giving of service to others.

Hints and hazards

Careful and thorough organization is a must, and this may mean some red tape and some obstacles in setting up the Scheme. Once these are overcome the benefits are enormous. The Scheme is an excellent means of drawing young people into your youth group and hence of bringing them into contact with Christianity. But don't let the means become an end in itself! The Scheme should be only a part of your group's programme.

Variations

It may be possible to adapt elements of the Scheme without actually participating in it. County stores make equipment available even to those groups which are not in the Scheme. However, a comparable standard of safety and training is essential. Also, contact an existing local Scheme and offer to help with arranging Service activities, etc.

PART 6
TO THE YOUTH GROUP – SHARING YOUR FAITH AT SCHOOL OR COLLEGE

Introduction

School or college will be one of the most difficult places where you will want to share your Christian faith. Even if the school is technically a Church foundation, it may well be that a large majority of your fellow students will know little about the Church or what it means to be a practising Christian. The same may be true of the teachers. Even though most schools should have daily Assembly, often this will not necessarily be a Christian act of worship.

It is therefore inevitable that you will feel reticent about the idea of openly sharing your Christian faith with your fellow students, since even your friends may join in the general ridicule which does often occur. It is indeed hard on your own, but there is a safety and a comfort in numbers. Even Jesus got together twelve people to help him. So part of the secret is to be bold and to show confidence. People will tease you, but often because they are themselves curious about what goes on in church and why you are involved with it, though they may well not admit to being curious. Many think that churches are only for old people, and it is easy for young Christians to be regarded as "Bible bashers". But if you hold your ground, many will come gradually to respect you, and they will be helped by your example as they explore the Christian faith.

It all depends on whether you have the courage to be a bit different. Be as natural and normal as you can with people. Do make sure that you've got lots of interests – if you only talk about church, then people will think you are a bore. Some people may say, "You're a goody-goody to go to church." Don't try to be superior just because you're a Christian. Jesus welcomed everyone to him with open arms.

So, how should you try to share your Christian faith with others at school or college? The following ideas are suggestions which may be worth considering. They all have their roots in the experience of Christians at schools in a variety of areas – but none of the ideas has to be adhered to slavishly.

The key is to be ready to adapt according to the situation of your school. What will work well for a church school may go down like a lead balloon in a state school. What will be possible in a boarding-school will be impossible in a day-school.

The most crucial factor in all that follows is probably having a supportive and sympathetic Head Teacher or Deputy Head Teacher, who is willing to back you in all you would like to do in school. The increasing pressure of the school timetable can mean that extra activities are not given high priority. If the school authorities are not supportive, you might consider asking a local minister to talk with the Head.

Acknowledgements

All of these ideas have been carried out in schools of one sort or another, most notably the Beacon School, Banstead, Surrey, to whom grateful thanks are proffered by the author. Ideas have also been forthcoming from the Anglican/Methodist 66 Youth Club of Epsom Downs and the Focus Youth Club of All Saints, Banstead.

Form a Christian Union

Method

Form a Christian Union group to meet in school time on school premises.

Numbers

There is no limit to the number who can join, but it is good if there can be a wide age-range of students involved. It will also be important to enlist the assistance of a teacher, who can if necessary liaise with the other staff. For some events, you may need to split up a large group into smaller groups.

Equipment

A comfortable room, preferably with easy chairs – it should certainly have enough chairs for everybody. Tea- and coffee-making facilities.

Preparation

Obviously the main need is to advertise the presence of a Christian Union. The group needs to meet at a time suitable to the majority of the school, ideally in school time, such as the lunch-break. In reality, you may need to make personal contact with others who you know to be Christians in order to form a nucleus in the first instance, so that you have a viable group for others who are reluctant enquirers to join. You'll need to form a planning committee to arrange the programme.

Cost

Just a nominal charge to cover cost of refreshments. If you are going to invite outside speakers, you need to ask if there is any charge. If there is, you could levy a charge on those attending, or you could organize a fund-raising jumble sale.

Action

The key to the success of a Christian Union is probably an interesting, varied programme. Allow time for coffee and chat, but your meeting time may be limited, so it is important to allow proper time for the activity and the follow-up discussion. Don't be afraid to ask for advice on planning your programme from your clergy or teachers or youth leaders. Bible studies, discussions on topics you want to talk about, outside speakers, games, competitions, Christian videos and musical meetings are just a few of the possibilities, according to the talents of those who are around. It is good to finish each meeting with a short time of prayer, perhaps led by a couple of members.

A Christmas party is a good idea. Perhaps you could invite non-Christian friends to it. You could organize some food and some silly games, and an outside speaker could talk about something in keeping with the party spirit. What about an outdoors meeting in the summer? Anything which relieves the boredom of break-time will attract folk. Arrange a weekend away for the group – that can often be a superb way of integrating people. Your Diocesan Youth Officer will be able to put you in touch with possible venues; there are Christian outdoor youth centres all over the country. Why not organize a group to go on your Diocesan Easter Monday Pilgrimage, or to attend a Christian youth event such as Greenbelt, Easter People or Spring Harvest?

Hints

In one state school, there was an active Christian Headmaster who would not allow a Christian Union in his school because there was a danger of it becoming "a Christian clique which would be divisive in the school". It is certainly important that your group is open and welcoming to all – and not derogatory of those who refuse to join. Remember, too, that members who are church-goers may be worshipping in very different Christian traditions, so don't exclude those who may be of a very catholic or evangelical background. A balance needs to be maintained to suit all the members.

When arranging the programme, make sure that any outside speakers know exactly when they are coming, where they should arrive and who will meet them. There is nothing more daunting to an outsider than a school! A letter of thanks afterwards will be much appreciated, whether or not expenses have been claimed. Encourage your Christian Union members to wear a "fish" badge on their lapels.

Evaluation

It is not easy to evaluate the success of a Christian Union – except in terms of its growth or decline. Nor is it easy to evaluate how such a group will help individual members in their spiritual growth as Christians. What it will almost certainly do is give confidence to each of you as you try to share your Christian faith with others at your place of education.

The School Assembly

Method

As an alternative to the teachers taking the morning Assembly, ask if a group of you can "have a go".

Numbers

Let us assume that the whole of the school is present. The age range could be 12–18 years.

Equipment

Courage and confidence!

Preparation

Do what you do well. Something good that lasts for 5 minutes is much more effective than something poor that lasts for 15. As the saying goes, "If you don't strike oil in 5 minutes, stop boring."

Cost

None.

Action

1.   Perform some drama, maybe using some of the sketches available from the Riding Lights Company or from Christian Aid.

2.   Dramatized readings of the Gospel stories can often be compelling.

3.   Compose a rap based on a Gospel story.

4.   Use the themes of the Christian year – e.g. Advent, Christmas, Epiphany, Ash Wednesday, Lent, Easter, Ascension, Pentecost. Even these major festivals may not be understood by all. Present the story in a simple way – the students may begin to understand the Christian message if it is presented from scratch.

5.   Organize a Harvest Thanksgiving Service. Encourage everyone to bring along goods, which can then be given to the elderly in the community – or have a collection for Christian Aid.

6.   Remembrance Sunday – use this to talk about the peace of the world.

Hints

Rehearse what you plan to do again and again. Be audible and visible. Don't attempt to ask questions, expecting answers from such a large group. You will always go down well if you do what you know will be interesting and understandable. Always aim at the youngest students present – and then, hopefully, all will understand!

Evaluation

You will certainly get reaction from your fellow students and from your teachers. If the Assembly has gone down well, you'll get the chance to do another one.

The Year/Form Assembly

Method

Again, ask your year head or your form teacher if you can "have a go".

Numbers

There will be at least 120 pupils in a year and about 30 in a form. They will be the same age as you.

Equipment

Courage and confidence. You will need a lot of guts to stand up in front of your friends and contemporaries.

Preparation

The same as the School Assembly – but you may be in a smaller room without a stage. Be prepared for freer reactions than will occur in the full school assembly – you may get the odd catcall!

Cost

None.

Action

Because your audience will be smaller you will be able to do a more personal talk or story or drama. What about telling the group how you became a Christian or what goes on at your church? – Tell your story as quietly and undramatically as you can, as they will listen to you. Arrange for your local minister to come in to talk

about "what a clergyman does". Be prepared to answer
questions. You could divide the class into smaller groups
and get them to discuss a topic or question such as "Why
people do or do not go to Church" or "Can you be a
Christian without going to Church?" Use a sketch or
dialogue to illustrate some aspect of the Christian faith.
Get the class to write down (anonymously) people or
subjects they might want to pray for, and then put all these
topics together as intercessory prayer.

Hints

It's probably better to organize this kind of assembly with
others, in case you might be singled out as the class
"religious freak". There is safety in numbers.

Evaluation

Reaction will probably come quickly. If your Year/Form
Assembly achieves nothing else, it will at least have got
people thinking and talking – and who knows what seeds
may have been sown?

Involving local churches

Method

To create a positive link between your school and the local churches.

Numbers

Restricted only by the size of the church building you are going to use.

Equipment

An accommodating and friendly minister!

Preparation

Good liaison/communication between church and school authorities. Finding a church which is big enough and near enough to the school.

Cost

You could offer to make a donation to the church's heating costs, but the minister may waive this.

Main activities

There are probably at least three main areas in which a local church can be used by the school: (1) the setting up of a lunchtime club for students, to be manned by church members; (2) the establishment of a lunchtime worship/ Communion service specifically aimed at students; (3) holding the school Christmas and Easter services at the church.

1.   The lunchtime club could be a place where students could relax in their lunchtime break, perhaps play snooker and table-tennis, if they are available, and purchase refreshments. Numbers would probably have to be limited to a specific age group. This should be open to all. Even just getting students inside a church for their leisure break can be a start. Maybe a short act of worship could start or finish the session.

2.   Sundays, for many people, is often a day of leisure or activity when the thought of going to church can be far down a person's list of priorities. Perhaps a short act of worship or a simple communion service can be arranged during one of the weekday lunchtimes.

3.   Many schools like to hold a Carol Service at Christmas, and some like to have a service to celebrate Easter. Perhaps the local church might be the right place to host such an event. This can either be for the whole school – perhaps in two "sittings" if the church won't accommodate everyone – or for the school and parents, on a more voluntary basis.

Hints

All these ideas could work at school, but there is something about holding such events out of school which gives them a special significance to students. It will be vital to hold a rehearsal for all involved and to check beforehand whether extra seating/car-parking is needed.

Variations

Why not see if your form could visit local churches of different denominations, to study the differences in tradition, belief and practice.

Evaluation

Establishing links between church and school will be invaluable and will have many benefits, giving students the chance to see inside and worship in a church building.

Charity fund-raising

Method

Arrange an event which demonstrates practical Christian caring, with the aim of both raising money and raising the school's awareness of the world's needs.

Numbers

Unlimited. Maybe a form or a year can get together to raise money.

Equipment

A suitable venue for the event – indoors in case of bad weather?

Preparation

Advertise the event. Gather the goods to be sold. Get permission to use school equipment, e.g. computers for games, pottery and craft equipment, etc.

Cost

Keep your cost as low as possible, so that all funds raised benefit the charity. Make sure that you, or the school, have adequate insurance cover for what you plan to do.

Action

This divides into two sections: which charities the money is to be raised for and how the money is to be raised.

1. The range of charities is endless. If a specifically

Christian charity is to be supported, then Christian Aid, for example, will supply information and advice. One of the best ways of raising people's awareness is to support a person who will send newsletters to the school in return for sponsorship – or why not agree to sponsor a child who is being educated? Alternatively, select one charity to support each year. Ensure that the money you are trying to raise is targetable. If, for example, you are raising money towards the cost of a Land-Rover, get a breakdown of the costs of the major parts, so that the students will know when the wheels or the chassis, etc. have been bought.

2.   Again, the methods of raising money are legion. Basically, you want the maximum number of people to come and spend the maximum amount of money. Sales – jumble or more upmarket events – are an easy way. Sponsored events are more tricky, since the person giving the money is not getting anything for it – except the satisfaction of helping a good cause. Barbecues, car-boot sales, summer fetes and Christmas markets are all good money-spinners – you'll need the help of parents if you get ambitious. A fund-raising disco – properly controlled – can be another way that involves everyone. A charities fair, run by a year group, is another way of getting lots of people involved. An easy and common way of raising money is for the school to have a non-uniform day, when students are charged for the privilege of not wearing uniform.

Hints

Cover yourselves so that you don't lose money. For example, make sure that you can cover the cost of hiring a disco by selling tickets. Make sure that you get proper receipts for all the charity money you send off.

Variations

Maybe a Charity Committee can be set up at your school. Ideas will then flow easily and will get official backing. At the very least, it is good if the school can get involved in Comic Relief or Blue Peter's annual fund-raising. What about organizing an end-of-term "It's a Knockout" between staff and students to raise money?

Evaluation

The amount of money raised will be your best barometer – and so will the amount of interest which is engendered. All this is just another means of showing in a practical, caring way what it means to be a Christian.

A prayer support group

Set up a group of students, parents and staff who will meet together to pray for the school and its members.

Numbers

6–20 is about the right size: any smaller, and it becomes too introspective; any larger, and it becomes unwieldy.

Equipment

A place in the school which is quiet, comfortable and undisturbed, and yet accessible for all who want to take part.

Preparation

Advertising, particularly amongst parents and in local churches which serve the school. Deciding on a regular place, day and time to meet, so that there is minimal confusion.

Cost

None.

Action

1. Begin by enabling people to relax, perhaps by serving coffee, and let them chat informally. Then, after ten minutes or so (to allow latecomers time to arrive), gather everyone around in an informal circle. Allow everyone the opportunity, if they wish, to mention any concern about the school, including specific people or events, but beware

of betraying confidentiality. Then have a time of quiet and allow members to pray in silence or aloud for as long as feels necessary. Close with the Lord's Prayer, or perhaps the school prayer, and the Grace together. Don't worry about silence – the group will speak or remain silent according to the spirit.

2.   Another way of leading such a group is to introduce a short Bible passage to discuss and then pray about. Some examples follow:

- *Read Matthew 5:13–16*. A Christian is called to be a light, to enlighten those who still live in darkness. Think about how you have been called to be a light in a dark world. How do you shine out to others? Discuss amongst yourselves how you can "shine out" at school.
- *Read Luke 9:23–27*. Some of you may feel that your cross is trying to be a Christian at school/college. Meditate upon what your cross is. Think about how you carry it. Are you easily ashamed of your faith – or are you actually quite proud that you are a Christian? Discuss and pray about how you should hold up your cross in such a difficult place as a school or college.
- *1 Corinthians 15:58 and 2 Corinthians 6:3–10*. The early Christians had to face a great deal of teasing and ridicule – and worse. Paul is here trying to encourage them to stick to their faith – not to be beaten by the taunts and gibes of others. Give thanks for the support you receive from other Christians in your school.
- *Read about the call of the first disciples: Mark 1:14–20; 2:13–17; John 1:35–51*. Take strength and encouragement from the fact that Jesus called "ordinary" people to be his disciples. They didn't have degrees in theology, nor were they people of great intellect or learning. They were just ordinary people like you. We often worry about what we should *say* – it's much more important that we should worry about what we *do* as Christians. One of the most important things we are called to do is to pray.

164

Evaluation

The fact that there is a group of adults and young people praying for the school will be an immense encouragement to all involved in the school – whether Christians or not.

Variation

Form a prayer partnership or a prayer triplet, so that two or three of you agree to meet regularly to pray for yourselves and for the school. Agree to remember the school in a moment of quiet at a set time each day – say midday – wherever you are and whatever you are doing at the time.

Rites of passage

Method

Encouraging awareness, thought and discussion about the place of the Christian Church at three important times in a person's life – birth, marriage and death.

Numbers

One or two form groups as a maximum, to allow for the active involvement of all in the discussions and the activities. This may form part of the PSE/General Studies Course.

Equipment

A friendly and willing minister. In the case of marriage, an optional extra is to provide clothes for the bride and the groom – but this is not essential!

Preparation

For the activity on marriage, it will be necessary to decide who is going to take which parts. Time is needed, since these activities will each take at least three double periods – and possibly longer.

Cost

None.

Activities

1. *Baptism*. A simple explanation by the minister of what is involved in infant baptism – perhaps a showing of the

short video, *Your Child's Christening*, produced by Kensington Church Videos. A discussion can then follow on what it means to be a Christian, what the role of parents and godparents is, etc. A visit to a church to see the font and/or baptistry can help – as can a simple explanation of the different baptismal practices adopted by the different Christian denominations.

2. *Marriage*. Here there is an ideal opportunity to "mock up" a wedding, to show what is involved in Christian marriage today. The room/hall can be divided up into two halves to simulate the church. All can take part as members of the congregation. A visit to a Register Office can help students to understand the difference between Christian marriage in a church and marriage in a civil ceremony. Discussion can also centre upon divorce – but beware of sensitive feelings here. It is wise not to enact the honeymoon!

3. *Funerals*. This is the rite passage which needs to be handled with the utmost sensitivity, for obvious reasons. And yet it should not be shirked, since all the group will experience bereavement of one sort or another, if they haven't already done so. The subject is probably best handled in a straightforward talk, with questions following. This could be given by a minister or funeral director who is sensitive to teenagers, especially those who have lost someone close to them. A simple explanation, without too much harrowing detail, of what happens to a body after death up to burial can help a great deal. A talk like this may provoke many deep questions about life after death, reincarnation and so on. Because students may be subdued by the subject-matter, it may be worth finishing the session with a question posed for discussion in small groups – for example, "What do you say to a friend who comes into school after the death of a close relative?"

Hints

Remember that different Christian denominations have different rules regarding baptism, marriage and burial. It can often help to set out the guidelines in a written hand-out so that there is no misunderstanding.

Evaluation

Since a large majority of the non-churchgoing population still turns to the Church for Christian baptism, marriage and funerals, these sessions – probably run over a number of weeks – will be of immense help to students as they begin to understand what an important role the Church has at the crucial stages in the lives of so many people.

Form a music group

Method

Form a Christian music group, using whatever talents the members have.

Numbers

Unlimited.

Equipment

A sound system will help, as will keyboards of some description.

Preparation

Someone needs to transpose the music suitable for the various instruments which are to be used.

Cost

Minimal.

Activities

1.   The group can gather together informally to learn/sing Christian songs, Taizé chants and whatever else appeals. There is some good Christian rock music which it may be possible to use. Music appeals to all ages, and it can be a very good medium to use to get the Christian message across to even the most apathetic of souls. You will find that you have a willing audience if you are able to perform occasionally – so long as you are good enough! Assembly is

a good time to perform, and so is lunchtime. What about performing at the school fete?

2.   Is your church putting on a Gospel concert? Why not ask the musicians to perform at your school during a lunch break? Even if this doesn't encourage your fellow students to come along to the concert, at least they will have heard the message which is being put across.

3.   How about putting your own new words to an old tune? It's not as difficult as you may think, and it's certainly easier to grab people that way than by putting old words to a new tune!

4.   Some songs which are popular in church may be new to your non-churchgoing friends. Give them an airing and prove that Christian music can be fun, exciting and tuneful.

Hints

Don't be too ambitious and overstretch yourselves. Keep within your limits and play only what you can play well.

Evaluation

You may be surprised at how popular your music group becomes and how much it is in demand.

Conclusion

The word "witness" comes from the Old English word "witan", which means "someone who knows and is therefore able to tell". The Church is made up of people who have been called apart by God to be his witnesses, to proclaim the Gospel (or the Good News) and to evangelize others.

There are no easy answers to the problems of sharing your faith at school or college. Indeed, it is probably the most difficult place of all in which to witness because, on the one hand, you want to be a witness to the Good News of Jesus Christ, and on the other hand, you don't want to lose friends or stand out in the crowd.

Discuss the problems of witnessing at school with other members of your church youth group. You may all be facing the same problems, even if you go to different schools.

Don't give up going to church to worship, and remember how much strength you gain from saying your prayers.

"Religion is caught, not taught." It is not so much by what you *say* as by what you *are* and how you behave that others will see Christ in you. It is said that other people will take much more notice of how you behave (54%) and how you look (39%) than they will of what you say (7%). Your behaviour will often be the best way of witnessing to your fellow students.

Finally, remember that big trees are grown out of small acorns. Don't worry if your efforts to share your Christian faith with your fellow students don't seem to be making any difference – they probably are. Let that fact encourage you and give you hope.

PART 7
FOOD GLORIOUS FOOD – WELL SOME LEFT-OVERS, ANYWAY!

Give away your food and your faith

Method

Choose a charity to which you can give food, then as a group set out to help them by collecting as much for them as you can. E.g. you could give to a local night hostel, to the Crisis at Christmas appeal or to any of the organizations which help the homeless.

Engaging in this sort of project will attract a good deal of attention and will provide plenty of opportunities for sharing your faith.

Numbers

You will need as many helpers as you can get, so encourage your group to ask their friends to help.

Preparation

1.   Print hand bills and make posters to advertise what you are doing, making sure that the name of your church and the name of your youth group appear on each one of them.

2.   Arrange a dropping-off point for food to be delivered to.

3.   Decide on a starting date and a finishing date so that the activities are confined to a limited time.

Cost

Nothing.

Action

1.   Advertise what you are doing as widely as possible so that everybody in the area hears about it.

2.   Start collecting food to give to local charities. Ask people to bring food into school or to drop it off between certain times at prearranged addresses.

3.   Then look forward to people asking you why, as a group, you have decided to do this sort of activity. You will be given plenty of opportunities to talk about your faith and your desire to help those in need.

4.   Always have something to give to people who ask who you are and why you are collecting, such as bookmarks with details of church services on them.

Hot cross buns and Easter eggs

Method

Hold a fun food evening at which you can eat hot cross buns and Easter eggs. Have it as near to Easter as possible.

Numbers

Each member of your group should bring 1 guest.

Equipment

Enough hot cross buns and chocolate eggs to go round.

Preparation

1. Organize some good warm-up games.

2. Prepare a short, punchy talk about the real meaning of Easter, using the buns and eggs to illustrate it.

Cost

This event will work out at approximately 60p per head. Your group members should pay for their guests.

Action

1. Welcome everyone in and start with a good selection of warm-up games. Use games that will encourage people to talk and mix with as many people as possible.

2. Enjoy a drink and some hot cross buns together, making sure that the conversation keeps flowing.

3. After this send them all on an Easter egg hunt. This

will be fun if you and your group are enthusiastic. You will have to have one rule, which is this: nobody is allowed to eat an egg until they have all been found and everyone is back in the main room.

4.   Present your talk about Easter and what it means to Christians. Talk about what Jesus did and about the new life he offers, using the crosses on the buns and eggs to illustrate your message.

5.   End by giving everybody an egg to eat and an invitation to your next meeting.

Maundy Thursday shared meal

Method

A simple shared meal in which the story of Jesus washing the disciples' feet is retold. This activity is best suited to those who are already in touch with the group rather than complete "outsiders".

Equipment

A home or a hall in which to hold the event. Candles and shaded lamps. A simple menu.

Preparation

Organize the venue, the food, the drama and the talk.

Cost

50p–£1 per head.

Action

1.   Create a warm, intimate atmosphere using candles, shaded lamps, quiet instrumental music, etc. Serve a simple meal, e.g. pasta and fruit, with water to drink.

2.   Start with a questionnaire entitled "Test your serve" – it should ask humorous/serious questions to get people thinking about what it means to serve, how easy or hard they find it, etc. Do this in pairs, sharing the results with the whole group.

3.   Eat the first course, serving each other. No one can

ask for anything to be passed, and no one can eat until everyone has all they need!

4.   Between courses have John 13:1–20 read as a dialogue. Then give a brief talk, drawing out these points:
(i) In washing their feet Jesus was being a servant to the disciples. What stops us from following his example?
(ii) The foot-washing was an illustration of Jesus' ultimate act of servanthood for us on the cross.

5.   While the talk is being given have one group member wash the feet of another. This should be done as drama, and it should have been practised beforehand.

6.   End with the question? "Lord, are you going to wash my feet too?"

7.   Sing "Meekness and Majesty" or some other suitable chorus. Remember not to choose one which says things which some of those present won't yet be able to say about commitment.

8.   Dessert.

9.   Anyone for washing up?!

Using the Church festivals

Method

Making good use of the main festivals, when many young people will think of coming to church.

Numbers

As many as your venue can take!

Equipment

A home, food and drink.

Preparation

Prayer and invitations.

Cost

25–30p per person. This could come out of your youth group's kitty.

Action

It is a good time to invite someone to church at Christmas and Easter. They will be more keen to come if they have a friend to sit with, and they will feel more at ease if there are a lot of young people at the service. The prospect of festive food afterwards makes the whole thing even more appealing! Serve mince pies, hot non-alcoholic punch, hot cross buns, coffee, etc., after the service, in someone's home. This is a very natural setting for group members to ask their friends, "What did you think of the service?" Some worthwhile conversations should develop.

Hints and hazards

Make sure that the service you are inviting the young people to will be appealing to them. Prime your group members to be ready to chat about more than the weather!

Variations

In one Anglican diocese All Saints' Eve parties have caught on as a positive alternative to traditional Hallowe'en parties. Lively worship celebrating Christ, the Light of the world (followed by food and fireworks), provides a setting for low-key evangelism.

DIY pizza party

Method

Spend an evening together making and eating pizzas.

Numbers

Numbers are restricted only by oven space.

Equipment

Ovens, baking trays, pre-prepared pizza bases and a variety of toppings.

Preparation

The pizza bases can be made up in advance in the baking trays. Alternatively, buy the bases ready made or use french bread. You can either buy the toppings or ask the young people to bring them. The basic pizza toppings are tomatoes and cheese. As for extra toppings, almost anything goes: sausage slices, ham, tuna, sweetcorn, peppers, pineapple, etc. Be sure to have a few "wild" toppings – e.g. chocolate sauce, M & Ms, strawberry jam, etc!

Cost

This varies between 50p and £1.50 per pizza.

Action

This evening is ideal for newcomers. Youngsters make up combinations of toppings either in groups or individually.

While the pizzas are in the oven games can be played. This evening works just as a social activity, or you could end it with an epilogue.

Epilogue

Aim to say who you are as a group and why you meet regularly. You might say something like this: "What does and doesn't mix? [Refer to some of the pizza toppings.] Some people say that the Christian faith and fun don't mix – but in this group we believe that they do mix! Why not come again and find out more about the group?"

Hints and hazards

The main problem is finding enough oven space. Beg or borrow some microwave ovens, or use a church hall with large catering ovens.

Variations

Potato fillings, popcorn toppings, a variety of ice-creams, etc.

Lunch is served

Method

Provide lunch either on a Sunday or on a weekday in Lent.

Numbers

Unlimited – as many as can be catered for. The best lunches are the ones where people do not have to book a place, but just turn up. But there are obvious dangers with this!

Equipment

Good catering facilities and a good dining area, with plenty of space for any latecomers.

Preparation

If you are providing a Lent frugal lunch, your menu could be soup, bread, and cheese, finishing with coffee. If you are planning a Sunday lunch club, something more substantial may be needed. Shepherd's pie and lasagne are ideal because they can be stretched to cater for all. Roast beef and two vegetables is ambitious!

Cost

Traditionally people make contributions to frugal lunches – you may like to suggest a minimum donation. For a Sunday lunch club, you will need to cover all your costs. You might want to build up a float, so that you can do something special at Christmas.

Action

1.   You will need a good band of volunteers who are prepared to help with the preparation. Your youth group may well be a ready, willing and able source of help, particularly on Sundays. A Sunday lunch club is often welcomed by those who live alone, of whatever age they may be. Families will also be grateful for a meal which is cooked for them, even if this happens only once a month. In one church, the lunch club became a haven for homeless folks: they knew that they could get a good, hot meal there once a month.

2.   Of course, providing food is not all that matters. It is also important that folk are given the chance to talk and to enjoy some fellowship together. So making sure that a few people are wandering round and chatting and making friends is as important as ensuring that you have enough people to help with the cooking.

Hints

1.   It is a good idea to make sure that everyone pays for their lunch – even those who are homeless, for they still have their pride.

2.   There is no reason why those who have enjoyed the food should not be asked to help with the washing up. Some good friendships can be formed that way!

Fondue quiz evening

Numbers

Limited to the number you can comfortably get round a table and who can get safe access to the fondue. Maybe get two tables together with two fondue sets.

Equipment

A fondue set, consisting of a saucepan (ceramic or metal), a stand for the saucepan, a fuel burner and as many fondue forks as you need.

Preparation

1.   You can either cook a cheese fondue (prepare this accurately according to the recipe), which is chunks of bread dipped in melted cheese, or you can cook chunks of meat in oil. This latter method is especially suitable, as it lasts quite a long time and everyone can cook their meat as it suits them. You might want to have both types of fondue.

2.   Heat the oil in the saucepan, place it over the flame, and it will stay hot for the whole evening. For the cheese fondue, prepare the cheese – melted according to the recipe – and it too will stay bubbling hot. Supplement the fondue with a salad and perhaps a baked potato. This will make an ample meal.

Cost

You can spend as much or a little as you wish. Make sure that you buy good-quality meat that can be cooked easily.

Action

The main point of the evening is to make your friends – and those you don't know quite as well – feel relaxed and able to enjoy each other's company. A quiz – perhaps of the "Trivial Pursuit" type – can add a fun element to the evening. Whenever someone answers a question correctly, they get a piece of meat or cheese-dipped bread. Prepare some questions on the Bible, if you want to add a religious flavour to the evening.

Evaluation

Has everyone had a good time?

A barbecue/faith picnic

Numbers

Unlimited.

Preparation

For a barbecue, sausages, beefburgers and something for the vegetarians will probably be enough; chicken and steak are more expensive but can easily be done. For a faith picnic, all you need to provide is a venue and perhaps some drinks for everyone.

Action

You will need dry weather! Make sure that any strangers are warmly welcomed and quickly integrated. For a faith picnic, everyone brings some food and shares it. At a barbecue, people can either cook their own food or, better still, have it cooked for them. The latter option gives them ample opportunity to meet old friends and make new ones. Encourage all your group members to bring a friend along. The event can end with a quiz or a video or games.

Barbecues and faith picnics are ideal for two youth groups to mix together, or for a church congregation to get to know each other better, or for outreach to new people in the area.

Evaluation

A great deal can be achieved just by giving people the chance to meet together. A social event like this can make all the difference to a group.

PART 8
MAJOR EVANGELISTIC
EVENTS

Introduction

Unlike fifteen or twenty years ago, we are now at a point in the life of the Church in general where congregations from different backgrounds are prepared to join forces to promote the Gospel and all that it stands for. Graham Kendrick has shown us this with the Make Way March and the March for Jesus, events that present the Gospel through music and unite the churches in a given area.

Ecumenical youth work opens up endless ways of increasing the links between churches. It also builds up the young people and their group leaders – a thing which most leaders will eagerly desire!

So often Christian young people hide away at school, thinking that they are quite an oddity, while in fact there are many others doing exactly the same. The most effective way of overcoming this obstacle is to bring church youth groups together: then schoolmates can meet as Christians and amaze each other. They discover that they have allies at school. Consequently a school Christian Union begins to develop and a caring network is set up.

Leaders of youth groups often battle away trying to put together an effective programme, until they begin to feel stale or unsupported. It is a good idea for the group leaders from the local churches to get together regularly to pray, share ideas and put on a major event occasionally.

Once young people get together, then adult congregations begin to interact more effectively. It will be necessary to involve adults in some events, so make sure that they come from different churches. In Acts 2:42–47 we read that the members of the church in Jerusalem joined together in each other's homes. Let us follow their example by uniting to present the Gospel of Jesus Christ to our young people.

Your ideas about holding a big event will change as time goes on. At the outset you may be very excited – you may believe that you can change the world! But a couple of weeks before the event is due to take place you may be panicking and wondering, "Will it ever actually happen?" All this needs consideration before you start, because if you pull out at the last minute it can be costly. We will take a look at finance later, but be prepared for some large bills.

What sort of event?

What sort of event do you want to hold? Will it be purely evangelistic – an opportunity to present the Gospel to young people in the area, then calling for them to make the decision of either inviting Jesus into their lives or rejecting him? Will it be a celebration – a fun event for those young people who already are Christians or who attend church groups? This needs to be decided at the start, because the preparations in some cases are quite different.

If you are considering an evangelistic event, then you have to think through how to gather non-Christian young people together. A mission to the local schools is a very good way of doing this. If carefully approached by a church leader, most schools will happily open their doors to a known team. There is normally a need for people to speak at assemblies; there may also be openings for lunch-time concerts and the possibility of taking some lessons. Schools need a lot of delicate handling, as some staff may feel threatened by a group of Christians coming into "their territory". Also, you must go in not to evangelize the young people but rather to inform them about Christ. Open forums – where members of the team leading the event have questions fired at them by the audience – are excellent starting-points. There is no evangelizing, just honest answers to questions. Maybe you could then consider having a few concerts at the end of a schools mission week, where more straight evangelism can take place.

Once you have decided what type of event you want to hold, you need to ascertain the length of time it will run for. It could last just for an evening or even for a whole week, but consider the stress factor if you are thinking about a week-long event. You must also consider where the event should be held. For a celebration for the present youth group members a church hall will be ideal, and this should hopefully keep the cost down. If you are aiming the event at non-Christians, then ideally it should be held on neutral ground such as a school hall or a village hall. This removes the pressure of being seen "at church" and creates a freer atmosphere. There will also be no arguments about which church the event should take place in!

Celebrations can be very successful if held outside, but remember that this is Britain – we can't always guarantee celebration weather! The noise factor must also be considered. You may have a big garden, but do all your neighbours want to celebrate with you? Perhaps they would rather watch *Coronation Street*! If you are holding the event indoors you need to make sure that the building you want to use will hold the numbers you may get, especially if you want to have some fun activities. You may need to obtain a music licence for the venue you choose. Ask your local police.

Booking your speaker

Big events don't happen quickly; they can often take a couple of years to prepare if they are to be done well. You will need to book your speaker or performers well in advance. For very well-known personalities, you will often find that the minimum booking period will be eighteen months ahead; more local speakers should have at least six months' notice. You should liaise with your speaker several times before the event: initially to decide on a

195

theme, and later to discuss staging and any equipment that you may need to provide. Allow a speaker a certain amount of flexibility, but also be fairly specific about your own requirements. Contact your Diocesan Youth Officer or your denominational youth co-ordinator for the names and addresses of good speakers. Consider local full-time youth workers – you don't always need to get the most well-known speakers in order to get the message across or to gather the biggest crowds.

Music

Young people today have developed a whole new musical culture, just as we did when we were teenagers. We need to be sympathetic to this when we consider the musical input. Professional bands will often be much more aware of this than will many of our own church bands, so think carefully before inviting a band to play at your event. Look around for local bands who may be good enough either to play for the whole event or to support a professional band. Be willing, though, to hire good sound equipment for them, as it is fairly unlikely that they will have it themselves. You may need to obtain public address equipment anyway, if you want your speaker to be heard!

When it comes to worshipping together, one needs to do some careful thinking before choosing songs. You will need to obtain a copyright licence. This will involve some cost, but it will not be as expensive as buying a book for everyone. You can then either display the songs by means of an overhead projector (not always so good if you are outdoors!) or print song-sheets. You may wish to use some songs which the licence does not cover. You simply can't use them unless you contact that particular company separately and get their permission. Once you have covered this legality you can get down to choosing songs. This task should be done with a member of the worship band. Don't just throw together a collection of your favourite "boppy" songs! Consider the theme and format of the event: e.g. praise songs to start with, quieter songs to help create an atmosphere of prayerfulness, etc. For more information please refer to Part 4 on the performing arts.

Once you have discussed staging requirements with those who will be performing you need to go about obtaining a stage! It may be that the local hall you are using has just what you require – if so, all well and good. If not, then you will need to hire a suitable venue. Let your fingers do the walking and pick up your Yellow Pages – at times like this it can be invaluable. Look up "Theatrical Supplies", and you should then find the necessary contacts for staging, sound equipment and also lighting.

Lighting

Whether indoors or outside, you will almost certainly need lighting. If you don't really know your requirements, consult a lighting company; they are usually very helpful. They may also try to supply you with more than you need, but you are the customer, so don't be afraid to say no! Costs vary, so shop around, and you may find that you can hire quite reasonably.

Publicity

In an age of technology we can no longer publicize an event simply by drawing a few posters and sticking them on the church notice-board. Our posters must be attractive to young people and must communicate effectively. Posters like this will cost a considerable amount, unless you know a professional, but good publicity is important. You may wish to ask the young people in your group what "grabs" them before getting your ideas printed – who better to advise you than the sort of people you are trying to attract? Go and speak to someone from your local newspaper. Also try your local radio station, if you have one. If your event is big enough you may get onto local television. When we are doing God's work we should be thinking along the lines of "nothing but the best" – and at times that costs money.

You may decide that small publicity handouts will be useful. These can be given out in schools or in your town centres but be sure to obtain permission from the relevant authorities first. Make these handouts similar in appearance to your main posters. Even if the young pople don't keep the handouts they will almost certainly glance at them, and when they then catch sight of a poster – bingo! It all raises their awareness of the event, and this increases the chances of them attending it.

Insurance

In your planning and preparation it is absolutely vital that you obtain adequate insurance to cover not only equipment but, most importantly, people. If equipment is hired, don't assume that it is automatically insured while in your possession – more often than not it won't be. Check with the suppliers well before you are due to collect the equipment or have it delivered. If insurance is required, ask them to give you a full costing list of the equipment, as the insurers will probably ask for this.

Regarding people, you will be advised by your insurers as to what cover is best, but usually public liability for £1,000,000 will be necessary. This may not be needed if you are using a hall which has its own insurance, but you can certainly never be too careful. You can also guarantee that if you don't cover yourself something will go wrong, so be prepared and it probably won't. The fact that you have prayed hard won't stand up in court as an argument against a lawsuit!

Stewards

The last thing you will want to worry about while the event is actually taking place is how the cars are being parked, whether or not there are enough seats and if those attending are acting in an orderly manner. You will therefore need a team of stewards, including a chief steward. He should be able to instruct his team members on the fire safety procedure, including showing them the emergency exits and the fire extinguishers. For all the stewards, safety is the name of the game. Those dealing with the car-park should wear yellow visibility jackets – your local police will advise you where to get hold of them. At night, torches are extremely useful for directing both traffic and people.

Walkie-talkies are fun toys but are also a very useful piece of equipment. You may decide that they are unnecessary if the site or building you are using is very small. However, if you choose to use them you will find them quite cheap to hire. Don't use too many, or confusion will occur, but aim to have one in each major area, e.g. the car-park, the entrance, the main hall or meeting area, the information desk and the first aid post. Also make sure that the chief steward and you, the event organiser, have one.

It will be necessary for the stewards to familiarize themselves with the whole premises. The main point of stewards is to keep seemingly minor operations running smoothly. However, remove them, and the event will begin to crumble. Make them feel special, especially if they have had to stand outside in bad weather!

First aid

A first aid post is essential. There is no better way to deal with an emergency than to have the necessary people on hand. Whenever a large group gathers there is a chance of injury or people fainting, etc. It is important that instant treatment is available. Contact your local St John's Ambulance or Red Cross group – they will be only too glad to help you. You may find that you have members of one of these organizations in a local church; if so, do involve them. Organizing an event of this size may give you a headache, so you might need a few paracetamol yourself!

Food

When Jesus found himself preaching to a large crowd he dealt not only with their spiritual needs but also with their physical needs. Food plays a rather major role in the lives of most people. Indeed, as you have doubtless noticed, we have dedicated a whole part of this book to the subject. So just as Jesus fed the five thousand (Matthew 5), we must consider how to provide food for the crowd at an all-day/week event.

If you know how many people will be attending, then think about using church members to cook and serve. Don't attempt to lay on *cordon-bleu* cuisine – you are aiming at young people who want straightforward meals. Buffet food is generally a winner, but again, don't be too flash.

If you are outside, then a constant barbecue is probably the cheapest and most versatile way of feeding the troops. Keep the sausages, beefburgers and vegeburgers cold in a cold-box.

Alternatively, use a small fridge powered by a generator, and keep it stocked with canned drinks too. If you are cooking for large numbers use an oil drum cut in half lengthways; place this on a stand and cover it with a wire grate.

To obtain food and canned drinks in large quantities go to your nearest cash and carry. If you don't already have an entrance pass, ask them if they will give you a temporary one. They are normally very obliging, but you may find that you have to spend a minimum amount of money and that it must be cash and not a cheque. As well as the food, the cash and carry may sell other useful items, such as badges for your stewards and officials.

Counselling

You may have decided to make your event a non-evangelistic one, but you will still need to provide an opportunity for counselling. The event may spark off questions in the minds of the young people, and possibly in those of a few adults; if these questions are to be dealt with effectively, they need to be answered there and then.

If your event is to be evangelistic, then you will need counsellors to help those who wish to respond positively to the Gospel message; they will also be needed to answer questions from those who aren't sure. Remember, counsellors are not there to make the decision for the counsellee; they are there simply to listen, to answer questions, to explain points arising out of the meeting or the literature being used, and finally to bring the enquirer to a point where he/she can make his/her own decision.

Counselling isn't a job for everyone – indeed, it is quite a special area and requires careful handling, which possibly means hand-picking your team. Your counsellors must be able to listen, firm in their personal Christian commitment, able to hold confidences and honest about their experience of the Christian faith. They can be of any age – don't simply look towards the adults in your congregation. You will find many excellent counsellors among your youth group members. Anyway, a teenager will often find it easier to talk something over with someone of his/her own age.

Whoever you choose to counsel, they must be prepared to have training. Even if they are experienced counsellors, refresher courses don't do any harm, and they can use their experience to help newcomers in the field of counselling. You should be able to find a local church leader or youth worker who will take on the task of training for you. Discuss with them what follow-up materials to use, such as *Journey into Life* booklets and Gospels. Be sure to have copies of these at the training sessions.

Follow-up

For effective follow-up you need to have some way of recording information received from the counsellee. Some form of card system is most useful, but it should be handled by one person only. All information must be treated with the strictest confidence and should not be made available for general circulation. Such a card may look something like this:

```
┌─────────────────────────────────────────────────────────────┐
│                    Follow-up information                      │
│                                                               │
│ □ Miss  □ Mrs  □Mr                                            │
│ Full name_____ Age_____         │
│ Address_____       │
│ _____ Post code_____ Tel. no.:_____  │
│ Tick one box: □ Acceptance of Christ  □ Assurance of salvation  □ Rededication │
│           □ Other – please specify_____        │
│ Religious background/denomination_____        │
│ Any church contact?_____        │
│ How invited to meeting_____        │
│ Student, where?_____        │
│ Address (if living away from home)_____        │
│ _____         │
│ Church (while student – if any)_____        │
│ Counsellor_____        │
└─────────────────────────────────────────────────────────────┘
```

The counsellor must request the permission of the counsellee before filling out the card and he/she should complete it legibly so that follow-up is made easy. The card should be handed immediately to the one person designated to deal with follow-up.

From the information given, a suitable letter should be sent out to each individual so that they know they haven't been forgotten. The letter should invite them to the first of a series of follow-up meetings which are designed to give practical teaching on how to grow as a Christian. Suitable material for these meetings would be along the lines of the "Growing More Like Jesus" course produced by CPAS (Church Pastoral Aid Society). The meetings should be quite informal and your counsellors should be encouraged to come along to provide a point of contact for the counsellees.

Follow-up should also be designed to link each person to a church – either one where friends go or a local church, if they don't already attend one. Ideally, it should be a church where at least one of the counsellors goes, again to provide a point of contact.

Finance

Finally, let's now look at the subject that brings the most worries to most people – finance! Sadly, there is no way of avoiding the inevitable bills, some of which could be quite large. Remember how in Genesis 22 Abraham trusted God, even to the point of being prepared to sacrifice his own son. God saw how Abraham continued to prepare as he knew he had to, and God then stepped in and removed the burden from Abraham and provided for him. So often we carry the burden of financing an event – we won't allow God to help. Abraham called that place where the Lord provided the sacrificial ram "The Lord Will Provide"; if we trust him, God will provide for us.

Here are some practical ways in which money can be raised, without having to do the usual sponsored events:

- Youth services in each of the local churches in your area – perhaps one every three months. Ask for the collections taken at those services to be donated to your events fund.
- Sports evenings, at a local school hall or sports centre. Charge a reasonable entrance fee and put the profit into your fund.
- Simply ask each church for a donation.
- Use ideas from elsewhere in this book. E.g. hold a food event and charge people for a meal.

Only you will know how much you need to raise, but

Schools Mission 1991 Provisional Budget

Administration costs
- Postage (100 letters) — 20.00
- Photocopying (prayer letters, etc.) — 100.00
- Telephone (calls by team) — 20.00
- Stationery — 30.00
- Badges (for stewards and counsellers) — 15.00 — **185.00**

Follow-up Material
- Handouts (Gospels, booklets and personal info. cards) — 310.00
- Literature nurture groups — 230.00 — **540.00**

Hospitality/catering
- Initial reception — 50.00
- Main meals for team — 120.00
- Board & lodgings inc. breakfast & packed lunch — 220.00
- Initial outlay (refreshments) — 100.00 — **490.00**

Publicity
- Handbills (2,500) — 50.00
- Posters (for event and follow-up) — 200.00 — **250.00**

Hire costs
- Hall (actual) — 380.00
- School halls – evenings (caretaker costs) — 120.00 — **500.00**

Travel costs
- Dudley to Godalming return (4 cars) — 600.00
- Local travel (25p/mile) — 100.00 — **700.00**

Miscellaneous
- Extraordinary costs of team — 50.00
- Contingency reserve — 50.00 — **100.00**

Donation to team
- To keep team on the road — 735.00 — **735.00**

Estimate total budget — **£3,500**

remember to pay speakers their worth. Bear in mind that they not only give time to come and speak at the event, but before that they spend a great deal of time in preparation.

Recently we held a schools mission week in our local area, with the assistance of a professional team. Here is the budget we used:

Don't try to skimp on costs – it just isn't worth it. If the event doesn't look professional, then the young people won't want to know. At the end, try to keep some money in a fund to finance future events. These need not be so big and ambitious as your major event, but they keep the young people together and help the churches to grow together too.

Form a committee

So that is what to do and how to do it; now we must look at who should do it and when it should be done! Before you have a complete breakdown at the thought of having to do so much, remember that great word which removes immense amounts of pressure – delegation!

A committee needs to be set up, including representatives from each of the churches which are to be involved. The committee members should be youth group leaders and certain people who can offer help in the areas not covered by the youth leaders.

The preparation for your event will take between eighteen months and two years, so the committee won't need to meet too regularly at first, but the meetings will become more frequent as the event draws nearer. Generally speaking, there are far too many committees involved in church life, so to have to form a new one probably makes you cower. To make it work effectively, only have meetings when necessary. Otherwise you will end up sitting round drinking coffee and talking about anything except the matter in hand.

It will be necessary for you to formulate your committee

to meet the needs of your event, but, as a guideline, here is the outline of an organizing committee that should cover every area of responsibility:

Chairman/administrator: someone with administrative skills and a vision for how the event will work.

Secretary: the Chairman's right-hand person, who will take on a great deal of the administration.

Publicity Co-ordinator: someone to gather the necessary artwork and get it printed.

Follow-up and nurture group: someone to organize the groups which will help new Christians to grow in the immediate future.

Outreach: someone to liaise with schools and anywhere else where contact with young people is possible.

Hospitality and catering: someone to look after any people in the team leading the event who need feeding and accommodation. This person could also be in charge of the refreshments at the event.

Prayer: someone to arrange prayer meetings, prayer letters, etc.

Stewarding: a Chief Steward to organize a team of stewards who will be on duty at the event. They may also be needed to shift equipment.

Treasurer: someone to think of ways of raising money and to administer the funds.

Sound, lighting and stage: someone to arrange the hiring, insuring and setting up of equipment.

Security: especially if you are holding your event outside, you will need a team to sleep with the equipment and to be alert during the event.

Media: someone to liaise with local papers, television, radio, etc. (this should ideally be someone with experience).

Over to you!

I now come to the point where I say "Over to you!" All the information I have given you has been tried and tested in various parts of the country and, as yet, it has never failed. Obviously, as I said earlier, you will need to adapt all this to exactly suit your own particular event. Begin well by praying to make sure that both you and God have the same plans.

Make sure that when you finish a major event you have a good holiday booked – believe me, you'll need one! You may expect that having done all the hard work before the event, you will be able to relax during the event itself. Don't be fooled – the mental strain of seeing a venture through is as exhausting as the actual work before it.

I wish every group every blessing in undertaking any major venture. If you are working wholly for God, the benefits to be reaped are immense. Watch both the leaders and the young people grow as God's kingdom is advanced.

Useful addresses

Mission Teams

Saltmine Trust, PO Box 15, Dudley, West Midlands DY3 2AN.

British Youth for Christ, Cleobury Place, Cleobury Mortimer, Kidderminster, Worcestershire, DY14 8UG.

Church Army, Independents Road, Blackheath, London, SE3 9LG.

The 40:3 Trust, 46 Asthill Grove, Coventry, West Midlands, CV3 6HP.

Publicity

Christian Publicity Organisation (CPO), Garcia Estate, Canterbury Road, Worthing, West Sussex, BN13 1BW.

Literature

Church Pastoral Aid Society (CPAS), Athena Drive, Tachbrook Park, Warwick, CV34 6NG.